P9-CEW-655

RIPLEY'S BELIEVE IT OR NOT! 20th Series

Weird, wonderful facts that will make you shake your head in disbelief.

This fascinating chronicle of incredible oddities, gathered from all over the world by the tireless Ripley staff, will convince you once again that truth is indeed stranger than fiction.

If you cannot buy your favorite **BELIEVE IT OR NOT!** POCKET BOOK at your local newsstand, please write to the nearest Ripley's "Believe It or Not!" museum:

175 Jefferson Street, San Francisco,
California 94133

1500 North Wells Street, Chicago,
Illinois 60610

19 San Marco Avenue, St. Augustine,
Florida 32084

The Parkway
Gatlinburg, Tennessee 37738

4960 Clifton Hill, Niagara Falls, Canada

Central Promenade, Blackpool, Lancashire,
England

RIPLEY'S BELIEVE IT OR NOT! 20th Series
is an original POCKET BOOK edition.

Other *Ripley's Believe It or Not!* titles

*Are there paperbound books you want
but cannot find in your retail stores?*

Ripley's Believe It or Not!

20th Series

PUBLISHED BY POCKET BOOKS NEW YORK

RIPLEY'S BELIEVE IT OR NOT!® 20TH SERIES

POCKET BOOK edition published December, 1972

This original POCKET BOOK edition is printed from brand-new plates.
POCKET BOOK editions are published by POCKET BOOKS, a division of
Simon & Schuster, Inc., 630 Fifth Avenue, New York, N.Y. 10020.
Trademarks registered in the United States and other countries.

L

PREFACE

Alcibiades Kirillos of Tripolitza, Greece, was the father of three sets of twins, born 20 years apart: 1864, 1884, and 1904. He was married three times.

Antonia Elas of Santarem, Portugal, following a quarrel with her husband, confiscated his entire stock of trousers, all 20 of them. The husband searched in vain for the vanished garments. A friend of the family revealed that the wife was wearing all 20 of them under her hoopskirt! We should call her "The Woman who wore (all) the pants in the family."

A Uruguayan lake named "Twenty Bulls" was named after a herculean settler on its shores, whose strength was likened to that of 20 bulls!

When a Spaniard says, "Son las veinte" (It is 20 o'clock), he means, "It is much later than you think."

Professor Amadeo Frasanti of Florence was known as "Il Professore Devot^{mo}" for his strange habit of concluding all his letters with the two words "Suo Devot^{mo}" (abbreviated form of "Yours most devotedly") repeated 20 times in succession!

These five items all dealing with the Number 20 have been specially researched for use as an introduction to *Ripley's Believe It or Not! 20th Series,* which we are happy to launch herewith.

Again, after leafing through its contents, we recommend highly its wealth of *Believe It or Not!* material, which represents many years of research, enhanced by illustrations from the hand of Paul Frehm, our distinguished artist and Art Director.

It is a joy to sponsor this endless variety of incredibilities. As the book takes wing, we trust it will get the same enthusiastic reception as its 19 predecessors.

—Norbert Pearlroth
Research Director
BELIEVE IT OR NOT!

EMPEROR KAMEYAMA
(1248-1305) of Japan, RESIGNED HIS THRONE IN FAVOR OF HIS SON --CREATING A PRECEDENT FOLLOWED *BY 3 OTHER EMPERORS WITHIN KAMEYAMA'S LIFETIME*

THE **BELL** ON THE TOWN GATE OF ARBERG, GERMANY, IS STILL RUNG EACH EVENING TO COMMEMORATE THE FACT THAT A YOUNG WOMAN LOST IN THE NEARBY FOREST WAS GUIDED TO SAFETY **400** YEARS AGO *WHEN THE BELL RANG WITH NO HAND ON ITS CORD*

A **MASSIVE REPLICA** OF THE ANCIENT CROWN of BURGUNDY STANDS ON THE FLOOR OF THE CHURCH OF PAYERNE, SWITZERLAND --CONSTRUCTED FROM IRON REINFORCEMENTS SALVAGED WHEN THE BELFRY OF THE EDIFICE WAS TORN DOWN *IN THE 17th CENTURY*

A **STRANGE BEAST** APPARENTLY PART WOLF, FINALLY WAS KILLED NEAR MILAN, ITALY, IN 1728 -- *AFTER IT HAD SLAIN 12 CHILDREN*

7

EMPEROR AVITUS
(400-456)
WHO RULED THE ROMAN EMPIRE
FOR A YEAR, BECAME THE
BISHOP OF PLACENTIA, ITALY

THE TOWER
OF THE HOSPITAL CHURCH,
IN WINDHEIM, GERMANY, TILTS
14 INCHES OFF CENTER

THE REV. THOMAS SWIFT
WHO BECAME VICAR OF Goodrich, Wales, WAS DISINHERITED BY HIS MOTHER BECAUSE AS A YOUTH *HE ONCE STOLE SOME FRUIT FROM AN ORCHARD*

JOHANNES von WOVEREN
(1574 - 1612)
famed German linguist
SO CRAVED FLATTERY THAT HIS WILL BEQUEATHED $60 TO EACH FRIEND WHO WOULD PRONOUNCE A EULOGY AT HIS FUNERAL *PROVIDING EACH EULOGY CONTAINED AT LEAST 60 FLATTERING ADJECTIVES* AT HIS FUNERAL 22 FRIENDS DID SO, COLLECTING A TOTAL OF $1,320

GREENEVILLE, TENN.
IS THE ONLY TOWN OF THAT NAME IN THE COUNTRY *SPELLED WITH 4 E's*

THE **AEPYORNIS**
of Madagascar
A BIRD WHICH BECAME EXTINCT ONLY IN RECENT TIMES, GREW TO A HEIGHT OF 10 FEET, WEIGHED 1,000 POUNDS AND LAID AN EGG SO LARGE THAT ITS SHELL HAD A CAPACITY *OF 2 GALLONS*

LORD BALMERINO
BEFORE BEING EXECUTED IN LONDON TOWER TIPPED THE AXEMAN 3 GOLDEN GUINEAS *--AN ACT OF GENEROSITY WHICH SO UNNERVED THE EXECUTIONER THAT IT TOOK HIM 3 BLOWS TO BEHEAD BALMERINO*

THE NEBBIEN FOUNTAIN IN FRANKFURT-ON-THE-MAIN, GERMANY WAS CARVED OUT OF JUST **2 SOLID BLOCKS OF MARBLE**

THE OPERA STAR WHO GOT HIS INITIAL VOICE TRAINING AS A PEDDLER
ÉTIENNE LAINÉ (1747-1822)
A VEGETABLE PEDDLER IN PARIS, FRANCE, CAME TO THE ATTENTION OF THE DIRECTOR OF THE ROYAL ACADEMY OF MUSIC IN 1774 WHEN HIS SHOUTS OF "BUY MY ASPARAGUS" *SHATTERED A WINDOW IN THE DIRECTOR'S OFFICE*
THE PEDDLER BECAME A STAR TENOR FOR THE PARIS OPERA

STAGS WHICH DO NOT SHED THEIR HORNS ANNUALLY DEVELOP A GROWTH THAT LOOKS LIKE **A TOUPEE**

SCHOOLCHILDREN of the Berber Tribe of Southern Morocco, HAVING NO BLACKBOARDS, WRITE THEIR LESSONS IN INK ON SMOOTH CYPRESS BOARDS-- *WHICH CAN BE WIPED OFF AND USED AGAIN AND AGAIN*

THE **KLEMANTANS** of Borneo BURY THEIR DEAD IN COFFINS PLACED ON TOP OF A TALL POST -- WHICH IS DECORATED WITH *THE DECEASED'S CHINA PLATES*

THE **3d DUKE OF BRIDGEWATER** 1736-1803 ANGERED BECAUSE HIS FIANCÉE REFUSED TO SPURN HER SISTER, BROKE OFF THEIR ENGAGEMENT AND *NEVER AGAIN SPOKE TO ANY WOMAN FOR THE REMAINING 44 YEARS OF HIS LIFE*

SEOSES GRAND VIZIER OF KING KABADES of Persia (487-530) WAS EXECUTED BECAUSE HE *INSISTED UPON GIVING HIS DEAD WIFE A PROPER BURIAL* THE PERSIANS OF HIS TIME EXPOSED BODIES TO THE VULTURES

THE BENDER INN

NEAR CHERRYVALE, KANSAS, WAS AN ISOLATED TAVERN IN WHICH AT LEAST A DOZEN TRAVELERS WERE MURDERED *BY THE INNKEEPER, HIS WIFE AND DAUGHTER*

A **GUN** INVENTED IN GERMANY DURING WORLD WAR II *ACTUALLY COULD SHOOT AROUND A CORNER*

THE **ELECTRIC CATFISH**

IS STILL A MYSTERY TO SCIENTISTS ALTHOUGH DRAWINGS OF IT APPEAR ON THE STEPS OF THE SAKKARA PYRAMID -- *BUILT IN EGYPT 5,000 YEARS AGO*

ELIAS CADENET (1156-1280) OF PROVENCE, FRANCE, A CELEBRATED TROUBADOUR, WANDERED FROM CASTLE TO CASTLE SINGING HIS LOVE SONGS *FOR 100 YEARS*

THE **CHURCH** of the **IMMACULATE CONCEPTION**, Cincinnati, Ohio, WAS BUILT BY ARCHBISHOP PURCELL IN FULFILMENT OF A VOW HE MADE ON A VOYAGE FROM EUROPE *WHEN IT WAS FEARED THE VESSEL WOULD FOUNDER IN A STORM*

NATIVES of RAS HAFUN, SOMALILAND, WRAP WATER BOTTLES IN STREAMERS HANGING FROM THEIR TURBANS IN THE BELIEF THAT EVAPORATION OF THE WATER *WILL KEEP THEIR HEAD COOL*

7 CHURCHES BUILT SIDE BY SIDE IN MONSELICE, ITALY, BY THE DUODO FAMILY IN MEMORY OF THE 7 BASILICAS OF ROME

A **MANUSCRIPT** IN THE LIBRARY OF A MONASTERY IN OTTOBEUREN, GERMANY, WRITTEN IN 1200, CONTAINS THE *EARLIEST KNOWN USE OF ARABIC NUMERALS IN THE WESTERN WORLD*

SCLEROCRANGON JACQUETI a crustacean HAS ANTENNAE **3** TIMES AS LONG AS ITS BODY

William FITZHARDING
(1785-1857)
WAS MADE EARL
of FITZHARDING
AS A REWARD
FOR HIS EFFORTS
IN GETTING
*ALL FOUR OF
HIS BROTHERS
ELECTED TO
THE BRITISH
PARLIAMENT IN
THE SAME YEAR*
(1841)

THE **FIRST ACT OF SUBMARINE WARFARE**
WAS PERFORMED 2,450 YEARS AGO
BY A WOMAN.
CYANA, A GREEK GIRL, DIVED INTO THE
SEA WHEN PERSIAN KING XERXES I
INVADED HER COUNTRY--SHE CUT THE
CABLES OF THE ENEMY SHIPS--CAUSING
MANY TO FOUNDER ON THE REEFS

THE BELLS of ST. MARY
of Enda Mariam, Ethiopia,
ARE MERELY STONES HUNG
BY ROPES, AND THEIR
MUSICAL SOUNDS ARE MADE
*BY STRIKING THE ROCKS
WITH A WOODEN HAMMER*

HORSE CARTS
in Mongolia
ARE CONSTRUCTED
*WITHOUT A
SINGLE NAIL*

THE **GREAT-EARED NIGHTJAR** of Malaya, UTTERS AS A LOUD, CLEAR, MELODIOUS CRY *"DRINK THE BEER"*

THE **EGGS** OF THE YELLOW HAMMER ARE MARKED WITH WHAT APPEARS TO BE *RANDOM SCRIBBLING*

Edward WINSLOW IS THE ONLY MAYFLOWER PASSENGER OF WHOM AN AUTHENTIC PORTRAIT STILL EXISTS

ADOLF DIENSTAG

(1870-1918) of Brno, Czechoslovakia, WHOSE NAME IN GERMAN MEANS **TUESDAY** WAS BORN ON A **TUESDAY** WAS MARRIED TWICE ON **TUESDAY** TWICE BECAME A WIDOWER ON **TUESDAY** *AND DIED ON A TUESDAY*

PANCAKE ROCK ON THE **KENTUCKY RIVER** A SERIES OF PANCAKE-SHAPED ROCKS RISING **75 FEET** IN THE AIR *STANDS ON A BASE* ONLY **4 FEET BY 6 FEET**

15

THE PERGOLA IN MOUNT STORM PARK, IN CINCINNATI, OHIO, IS AN EXACT *DUPLICATE OF THE TEMPLE OF LOVE IN TRIANON PARK, IN VERSAILLES, FRANCE*

HUSBANDS and **WIVES** in India WHO DESIRE CHILDREN *WHISPER THEIR WISH INTO THE EAR OF A SACRED COW*

The **UPSIDE-DOWN FISH** (Synodontis nigriventris) A CATFISH THAT ALWAYS *FLOATS UPSIDE DOWN*

MEN OF THE WA-POKOMO TRIBE OF THE TANA RIVER REGION, EAST AFRICA, ARE NOT CONSIDERED QUALIFIED TO MARRY *UNTIL THEY HAVE KILLED A CROCODILE*

THE COLUMBIA RIVER LIGHTSHIP #50
BLOWN ASHORE AT THE MOUTH OF THE
COLUMBIA RIVER ON NOV. 28, 1899, COULD
ONLY BE REFLOATED BY TRANSPORTING
IT OVERLAND FOR A MILE TO BAKER'S BAY,
*A TREK THROUGH LOOSE SAND, WOODS
AND HILLS THAT REQUIRED 3 MONTHS*

JACOPO PICCININO
(1423-1465)
ITALIAN ARMY LEADER
INVITED BY KING
ALFONSO TO BE HIS
GUEST OF HONOR IN
NAPLES, WAS FETED
FOR 27 DAYS
-- *THEN EXECUTED*

THE **DOEDICURUS**
PREHISTORIC ANCESTOR
OF THE ARMADILLO
IS STILL FOUND IN FOSSIL
FORM IN SO. AMERICA BY
NATIVES WHO USE ITS
ARMOR *AS A BATHTUB*

THE **SUCKER FISH** of Borneo

A WEAK SWIMMER, KEEPS ITSELF
FROM BEING SWEPT DOWNSTREAM

*BY PLASTERING ITSELF AGAINST
A ROCK WITH THE BROAD
ADHESIVE SIDE OF ITS BODY*

TOAD ROCK
Mount Abu,
India,
*NATURAL
STONE
FORMATION*

17

2 RIVERS THE ISOLE AND THE ELLE, JOIN NEAR QUIMPERLÉ, FRANCE, BUT BECAUSE THEY ARE SO EQUAL IN SIZE, *BOTH LOSE THEIR IDENTITY AND MERGE AS THE LAITA RIVER*

AN **EGG** FOUND BY JOSEPH CROCKETT, of Danville, Maine, *ACTUALLY COMPRISED 5 COMPLETE EGGS* -- ONE INSIDE THE OTHER

ABASSA

SISTER OF HARUN-AL RASHID, THE CALIPH OF THE ARABIAN NIGHTS, WAS BANISHED TO A LIFE OF POVERTY BY HER BROTHER *BECAUSE SHE BECAME THE MOTHER OF A SON --WHO MIGHT HAVE BEEN A LEGAL HEIR TO THE CALIPH*

THE **NOSSEN TOWN CHURCH,** Germany, BUILT IN 1563, TOOK AS ITS MAIN ENTRANCE THE PORTAL TO THE DINING ROOM OF THE ALTZELLA MONASTERY *--WHICH COLLAPSED INTO A COMPLETE RUIN IMMEDIATELY AFTER REMOVAL OF ITS DOOR*

THE MODEL HUSBAND
GOUVERNEUR MORRIS (1752-1816) WHO MARRIED ANNE CAREY RANDOLPH WHEN HE WAS 57 AND SHE WAS MANY YEARS HIS JUNIOR, PROVIDED IN HIS WILL THAT IF SHE SHOULD REMARRY *HER INCOME WOULD BE DOUBLED*

THE RHETASSA HEREDITARY WELL CLEANERS OF THE SAHARA DESERT, OFTEN ARE LOWERED TO A DEPTH OF 160 FEET TO REMOVE SAND FROM THE BOTTOM OF WELLS -- *AND REMAIN UNDERWATER WITHOUT AIR FOR AS LONG AS 3 MINUTES*

ALEXANDER DUMAS Jr. (1824-1895) WHO ALSO BECAME AN AUTHOR, FREQUENTLY TOOK WALKS WITH A PET *VULTURE ON A LEASH*

THE TOWN of DUIRAT
in Southern Tunisia
IS ENTIRELY LOCATED
INSIDE A SINGLE MOUNTAIN

IF A YOUNG TWIN DIES
IN THE YORUBA TRIBE
of Nigeria, Africa,
THE SURVIVOR MUST CARRY
AROUND A WOODEN STATUE
OF THE DEAD TWIN
—*WHICH IS CLOTHED LIKE THE
SURVIVING TWIN EVERY DAY
AND GIVEN THE SAME FOOD*

Bats OFTEN
COME TO REST
ON THE BACKS OF
BULLFROGS–WHICH
*SEEM TO OFFER
NO OBJECTION*

CHARLES BEVERUNG DRUMMER BOY ON THE SHIP "LADY ELGIN" WHICH SANK WITH A LOSS OF 297 LIVES IN LAKE MICHIGAN *SAVED HIMSELF BY SWIMMING TO SHORE - USING HIS DRUM AS A LIFE PRESERVER!* (Sept. 8, 1860)

THE **BELLS** of the Church of Jever, Germany, WERE ORDERED RUNG NIGHTLY IN 1575 TO GUIDE HOME THE CITY'S 75-YEAR-OLD RULER, MARIA, WHO HAD MYSTERIOUSLY DISAPPEARED— *THEY HAVE BEEN RUNG EVERY NIGHT FOR 389 YEARS*

A **HIGH-LEVEL GREETING** THE **WATUSI** of Ruanda, Africa, HONOR ANY GUEST BY RACING TOWARD HIM -- *AND THEN HIGH JUMPING OVER HIS HEAD*

BEER MUGS GIVEN TO THEIR BOY FRIENDS BY GIRLS IN 16th-CENTURY FINLAND WERE ELABORATELY CARVED SO IT WOULD BE *DIFFICULT TO DRINK FROM THEM*

VINCENT HALLINAN

AN ATTORNEY of San Francisco, Calif., PLAYED RUGBY IN A REGULAR MATCH WITH THE SAN FRANCISCO "BATS" CHAMPIONSHIP TEAM CONTINUOUSLY FOR NEARLY 30 MINUTES *AT THE AGE OF 73* (March 7, 1970)

THE BAPTIST CHURCH OF MOUNT VERNON
Wisconsin
ERECTED IN 1869 FOR YEARS WAS OPENED ONLY FOR FUNERAL SERVICES FOR A MEMBER OF ITS ORIGINAL CONGREGATION *IT NOW IS USED ONLY ONCE A YEAR FOR A MEMORIAL SERVICE*

THE TULIP PULPIT
in the Cathedral of Freiberg, Germany, CONSTRUCTED IN THE SHAPE OF A FLOWER IN 1510, WAS USED ONLY ONCE BECAUSE THE PASTOR WHO DELIVERED THE FIRST SERMON FROM IT *DIED OF A STROKE*

THE LONG-HORNED GRASSHOPPER
of South Africa
ESCAPES PREDATORS BY *RESEMBLING A TOBACCO LEAF*

22

THE **GIANT CRICKET** of Africa WHICH GROWS TO A LENGTH OF 2 INCHES *LIKES TO EAT HUMAN HAIR*

THE **HOLY WATER RECEPTACLE** OF THE CHURCH OF ST. SULPICE, IN PARIS, FRANCE, IS A HUGE SEA SHELL BROUGHT BACK FROM THE ORIENT BY A PILGRIM CENTURIES AGO

TS'AO TS'AO
(155 - 220)
FATHER-IN-LAW OF A CHINESE EMPEROR, RULED THAT THE OWNER OF A HORSE THAT TRAMPLED A FIELD OF GRAIN MUST DIE —*AND WHEN HIS OWN HORSE STRAYED INTO A GRAIN FIELD SENTENCED HIMSELF TO BE EXECUTED*
ON THE DAY HE WAS TO DIE FRIENDS PERSUADED HIM TO SETTLE FOR **HAVING HIS HAIR CUT OFF INSTEAD OF HIS HEAD**

KAFUR al AKSHID (903 - 968) WHO WAS PURCHASED AS A SLAVE BY THE SULTAN OF EGYPT FOR ONLY **18** GOLD PIECES, BECAME SULTAN HIMSELF AND RULED EGYPT FOR 23 YEARS *HE MADE USE OF THE NUMBER 18 BY ANY OF HIS SUBJECTS A CRIME PUNISHABLE BY DEATH*

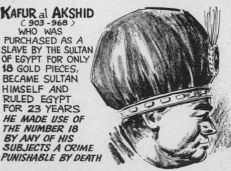

A **SQUIRREL** CAN CLIMB A TREE FASTER THAN IT CAN RUN ON *LEVEL GROUND*

23

THE CHURCH of PIERRELONGUE in France, WAS BUILT ATOP THE HUGE ROCK FROM WHICH THE VILLAGE DERIVED ITS NAME, TO ASSURE *THE LANDMARK'S PRESERVATION*

CHINESE HUNTERS

IN ANCIENT TIMES BAGGED WATER FOWL BY DONNING A HELMET AND A HUGE COLLAR WHICH ENABLED THEM TO FLOAT CLOSE TO THE BIRDS UNDETECTED *AND SEIZE THE FOWL BY HAND*

THE HOLY WATER VESSEL IN THE CHURCH OF LLANIDAN, WALES *REFILLS ITSELF FROM HIDDEN SPRINGS*

IT IS REFILLED FASTEST WHEN THE DAY IS HOT AND DRY

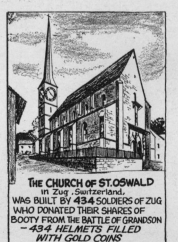

THE CHURCH OF ST. OSWALD in Zug, Switzerland, WAS BUILT BY **434** SOLDIERS OF ZUG WHO DONATED THEIR SHARES OF BOOTY FROM THE BATTLE OF GRANDSON —**434** HELMETS FILLED WITH GOLD COINS

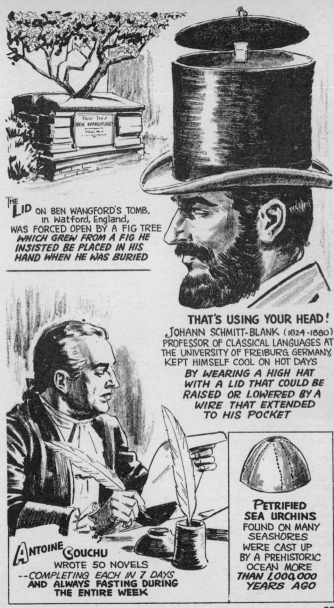

THE LID ON BEN WANGFORD'S TOMB, in Watford, England, WAS FORCED OPEN BY A FIG TREE *WHICH GREW FROM A FIG HE INSISTED BE PLACED IN HIS HAND WHEN HE WAS BURIED*

THAT'S USING YOUR HEAD! JOHANN SCHMITT-BLANK (1824-1880) PROFESSOR OF CLASSICAL LANGUAGES AT THE UNIVERSITY OF FREIBURG, GERMANY, KEPT HIMSELF COOL ON HOT DAYS *BY WEARING A HIGH HAT WITH A LID THAT COULD BE RAISED OR LOWERED BY A WIRE THAT EXTENDED TO HIS POCKET*

ANTOINE COUCHU WROTE 50 NOVELS --COMPLETING EACH IN 7 DAYS AND ALWAYS FASTING DURING THE ENTIRE WEEK

PETRIFIED SEA URCHINS FOUND ON MANY SEASHORES WERE CAST UP BY A PREHISTORIC OCEAN MORE *THAN 1,000,000 YEARS AGO*

THE RAILROAD TRACKS in Assam, India, WERE TWISTED OUT OF SHAPE BY AN EARTHQUAKE --WHICH ALSO SHORTENED THE RIGHT OF WAY ON WHICH THE TRACKS HAD BEEN LAID BY 3 FEET (June 12, 1897)

MARIE COTTIN (1773-1807) WHO HAD BEEN OUTSPOKEN IN CRITICIZING WOMEN AUTHORS HAD TO RAISE $250 TO RESCUE A FRIEND FROM DEATH IN THE FRENCH REVOLUTION --AND DID IT BY WRITING A NOVEL SHE FOUND IT NECESSARY TO WRITE 3 MORE BOOKS TO HELP FRIENDS--AND ALL FOUR WERE CRITICALLY ACCLAIMED

CANNON ONCE USED AGAINST AMERICAN SHIPPING BY CANADIAN PRIVATEERS ARE EMBEDDED, MUZZLE DOWN, ON STREET CORNERS IN LIVERPOOL, N.S. -SYMBOLIZING THE FACT THAT THE 2 COUNTRIES ARE NOW GOOD FRIENDS

HERE LIES OUR SON DEAD SOMEBODY STRUCK HIM ON THE HEAD

EPITAPH on the grave of PETER BAKER IN DEER PARK CHURCHYARD, Smallwood, Md.

WILLIAM RANDALL (1858-1947)
LIVED FOR **74** YEARS IN A PRIMITIVE CABIN ON COW CREEK, AN ARM OF THE YELLOWSTONE RIVER, Montana, *YET HE WAS NEVER SICK A DAY OF HIS LIFE FOR 89 YEARS*

BERBER WOMEN OF Southern Morocco WHO CONSIDER IT UNDIGNIFIED TO BEND DOWN AT THEIR WORK *WASH THEIR LAUNDRY WITH THEIR FEET*

THE **LEANING TOWER** of **BRUGES**, Belgium, IS **3** FEET, **11** INCHES OFF CENTER -- *AND TILTING MORE EACH YEAR*

THAT CHERRY TREE OF LUSCIOUS FRUIT BEGUILED HIM TOO HIGH. A BRANCH DID BREAK AND DOWN HE FELL AND BROKE HIS NECK AND DIED

Epitaph ON THE GRAVE of ANDREW C. HAND in Mount Pleasant Cemetery, Newark, N.J.

BARBARA MAISIAK and **RICHARD LIONELLO** BOTH OF CHICAGO, ILL., CASTING TOGETHER AT AXEHEAD LAKE *SIMULTANEOUSLY HOOKED THE SAME FISH* Sept. 20, 1970

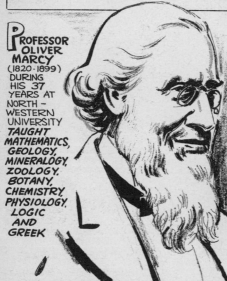

PROFESSOR OLIVER MARCY (1820-1899) DURING HIS 37 YEARS AT NORTH-WESTERN UNIVERSITY *TAUGHT MATHEMATICS, GEOLOGY, MINERALOGY, ZOOLOGY, BOTANY, CHEMISTRY, PHYSIOLOGY, LOGIC AND GREEK*

THE SMOKY JUNGLE FROG of the So. American jungles, WEIGHS ONLY ONE POUND -YET IT CAN SWALLOW A SNAKE 4½ FEET LONG

ARABIAN WOMEN of Chad, Africa, FORBIDDEN TO RIDE HORSES, *ALWAYS RIDE OXEN— ONLY THEIR HUSBANDS RIDE HORSES*

THE **TENT**

OF GENGHIS KHAN, WHICH BECAME THE MONGOLIAN EMPEROR'S TOMB IN 1227, IS STILL PRESERVED IN THE MUSEUM OF EDSHEN NORO, MONGOLIA -- *ALTHOUGH THE COFFIN IT SHELTERED WAS DESTROYED BY REBELLIOUS SOLDIERS*

THE **GIRL** WHO CONNED A KING

Jeanne de Choisy (1604-1662) WAS ON THE PAYROLL OF KING LOUIS XIV OF FRANCE FOR 18 YEARS TO CHAT WITH HIM TWICE EACH WEEK BECAUSE HE BELIEVED HER WHEN SHE ASSURED HIM:

"THE MORE YOU TALK TO ME THE MORE I CAN MAKE YOU AN HONEST MAN"

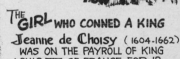

ANTON EDUARD **WOLLHEIM**

(1810-1884) OF HAMBURG, GERMANY POET, SOLDIER, NEWSPAPER EDITOR AND COLLEGE PROFESSOR *MASTERED 33 LANGUAGES*

A **CAVE**
NEAR BLAUBEUREN, GERMANY, HAS AN ENTRANCE SHAPED *LIKE THE FRAME OF A PAIR OF SPECTACLES*

THE CRESTED SCREAMER of So. America HAS **2** HUGE SPURS ON EACH WING

JOHN SELON
ALTHOUGH BLINDED BY AN EXPLOSION AS A BOY OF 15 IN 1920 *OBTAINED HIS LAW DEGREE AND BECAME A JUDGE IN BUTTE, MONTANA*

HOW TO CONVERT THIS CROSS-SHAPED CAKE INTO A PERFECT SQUARE WITHOUT ADDING OR DISCARDING ANY CAKE

Solution : CUT OFF THE SHADED PORTIONS AND USE THEM TO FILL IN THE AREAS MARKED "A"

THE **KOROTANGI** A SMALL SEA GULL CARVED OUT OF GREEN STONE WAS SO SACRED TO THE ANCIENT MAORIS OF NEW ZEALAND THAT ITS HIDING PLACE WAS ONLY KNOWN TO **ONE TRIBESMAN AT A TIME**

MANY NATIVES of New Guinea *NEED TO SHAVE ONLY ONCE—* A BARBER APPLIES A GUM TO THEIR WHISKERS AND REMOVES THE ROOT OF EACH HAIR --WHICH NEVER GROWS BACK

A **RAISED PARAPET ROAD** WHICH CROSSES THE SEA BETWEEN BRITTANY, FRANCE, AND THE ISLAND OF ST. CADO, *WAS BUILT BY THE IRISH ST. CADO 1,400 YEARS AGO--YET IS STILL IN EXCELLENT CONDITION*

THE **REV. DR. TIMOTHY DEWEY** (1771- 1850) ITINERANT PREACHER AND PHYSICIAN OF EAST HARTFORD, CONN.,

NAMED HIS CHILDREN:

ANNA DIADEMA

ARMENIUS PHILADELPHUS

ALMIRA MELPOLENA

PLEIADES ARISTARCUS

OCTAVIA AMMONIA and

ENCYCLOPEDIA BRITANNICA

2

HOW TO CHANGE THIS "**2**" INTO TWO OTHER NUMBERS WITH A SINGLE LINE

Solution:

2

DRAWING A FRAME AROUND IT CHANGES THE "2" INTO A "6" OR A "9"

A **FIELD CRICKET** HAS ITS EARS IN ITS FRONT LEGS *AND CHIRPS BY RUBBING ITS WINGS TOGETHER*

MOVE THE PICTURE TOWARD YOUR FACE AND THE MAN WILL DRINK THE WATER

THE TOWN THAT IS A BAROMETER
HUGH TOWN
CAPITAL OF ENGLAND'S SCILLY ISLANDS-
ITS HOUSES ARE CONSTRUCTED ENTIRELY
OF GRANITE, AND NATIVES INSIST
*THAT IT WILL ALWAYS BE FAIR
WHEN THE GRANITE GLISTENS FOR
HOURS BEFORE A SUNRISE*

A **MONUMENT** TO SIR WILLIAM GODOLPHIN ERECTED IN THE CHURCH OF PAUL, ENGLAND, IN 1681 *STILL BEARS HIS ORIGINAL BREASTPLATE, SWORD AND RAPIER*

OSTRICH EGGS WILL SUPPORT THE WEIGHT OF A 280-LB. MAN

THE **GREEDIEST** WRETCH IN ALL HISTORY!

PHRAATES IV TO BECOME RULER OF THE PARTHIANS *KILLED HIS FATHER, ALL 30 OF HIS BROTHERS AND HIS OWN SON* (37 B.C.)

THE **MOLE CRICKET** of So. America HAS SUCH POWERFUL FRONT LEGS *THAT IT DIGS INTO RIVERBANKS WITH ITS FORELEGS*

THE **EUCHELIA CATERPILLAR** AVOIDS BEING EATEN BY BIRDS BECAUSE ITS BLACK AND YELLOW STRIPES *CONVINCE PREDATORS IT IS A WASP*

F FIND A 7-SIDED DESIGN Solution:

NATIVES of New Guinea WEAR CAPS MADE OF *SPIDER WEBS* — THEY ARE SO DURABLE THEY LAST A LIFETIME

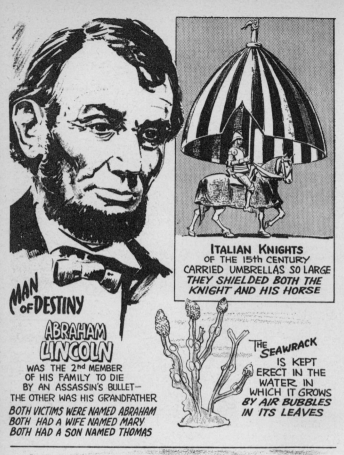

ITALIAN KNIGHTS OF THE 15th CENTURY CARRIED UMBRELLAS SO LARGE *THEY SHIELDED BOTH THE KNIGHT AND HIS HORSE*

MAN OF DESTINY

ABRAHAM LINCOLN WAS THE 2nd MEMBER OF HIS FAMILY TO DIE BY AN ASSASSIN'S BULLET— THE OTHER WAS HIS GRANDFATHER

BOTH VICTIMS WERE NAMED ABRAHAM BOTH HAD A WIFE NAMED MARY BOTH HAD A SON NAMED THOMAS

THE **SEAWRACK** IS KEPT ERECT IN THE WATER IN WHICH IT GROWS *BY AIR BUBBLES IN ITS LEAVES*

THE **EAGLE** near Quiberon, France, *NATURAL ROCK FORMATION*

34

THE FIRST RAILROAD IN AMERICA

A HORSE-DRAWN RAIL LINE WAS BUILT IN QUINCY, MASS., IN 1826 TO CARRY GRANITE FOR CONSTRUCTION OF *THE BUNKER HILL MONUMENT*

THE *REDUVIUS BUG* STALKS ITS PREY BY *COVERING ITSELF WITH DUST AND COBWEBS*

QUEEN MARGUERITE
(1553-1615) of France IMPROVED HER FIGURE BY WEARING *CORSETS MADE OF TIN*

THE SAUSAGE KITCHEN

A RESTAURANT IN REGENSBURG, GERMANY, HAS BEEN SERVING SAUSAGES AT THE SAME SITE SINCE 1146 *AN UNINTERRUPTED PERIOD OF 825 YEARS*

THE HUT OF ST. MAUDEZ IN MODEZ, FRANCE, CONSTRUCTED 1,400 YEARS AGO, FOR YEARS SERVED AS A MOORING FOR SHIPS AND *IS STILL SALUTED WITH A WHISTLE BLAST BY PASSING VESSELS*

LITTLE BOY WITH A BIG TITLE
PRINCE FREDERICK WILLIAM (1688-1740) of Prussia, WAS NAMED RECTOR MAGNIFICENTISSIMUS OF THE UNIVERSITY OF HALLE *AT THE AGE OF 7*

THE **DRACONIA RUSINA BUTTERFLY** of South America DISGUISES ITSELF AS A LEAF THAT HAS *BEEN DAMAGED BY DISEASE*

NATIVES of India WHO PRESS OIL FROM OLIVES DO SO WITH ONE FOOT IN A LINEN BAG HELD ABOVE THE POT INTO WHICH THE OIL DRIPS *-- AND MUST BALANCE THROUGHOUT THE DAY ON THE OTHER FOOT*

CHANGE THE 8 SQUARES TO 6 SQUARES BY MOVING 6 MATCHES
solution:

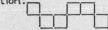

--AND THIS DIAGRAM TO 5 SQUARES BY MOVING 4 MATCHES
solution:

JAKOB LEHMANN
(1800 - 1863)
GERMAN PREACHER AND ASTRONOMER SUCCESSFULLY COMPUTED THE DATES FOR EACH EASTER *FOR THE NEXT 20,000 YEARS*

A **HUMAN SKULL** IS PLACED BETWEEN THE BRIDE AND GROOM AT WEDDINGS IN BORNEO AS A SYMBOL THAT *LOVE CAN OUTLAST DEATH*

DISCORD
5 TOMBSTONES ON THE HIGHWAY NEAR FALKENSTEIN, GERMANY, MARK THE GRAVES OF 5 MUSICIANS WHO PLAYED AT A DANCE IN THE 18th CENTURY AND THEN GOT INTO A FIGHT *IN WHICH ALL 5 WERE KILLED*

FISHERWOMEN of the Congo WEAR THEIR HAIR IN THE SHAPE OF THE *FISHING NETS WITH WHICH THEY WORK*

THE BRIARE SHIP CANAL Briare, France, CROSSES THE LOIRE RIVER BY MEANS OF A BRIDGE 2,172 FT. LONG *BUILT BY GUSTAVE EIFFEL OF THE EIFFEL TOWER FAME*

THE BELL ANIMAL [Vorticella] ATTACHES ITSELF TO A WATER WEED *AND APPEARS TO BE A TINY BELL FLOWER*

HORSESHOES WHICH COVER THE DOOR OF THE CATHEDRAL OF ST. MARTIN, IN CHABLIS, FRANCE, ARE FROM CRIPPLED ANIMALS WHOSE OWNERS HOPE THE SAINT WILL HEAL THEIR MOUNTS--*THE FIRST SUCH OWNER HAVING BEEN JOAN OF ARC*

PLINIUS SECUNDUS (23-79) THE CELEBRATED ROMAN HISTORIAN WROTE A 20-VOLUME "HISTORY OF THE GERMANIC WARS" *AS THE RESULT OF A DREAM* IN HIS DREAM HE WAS ASKED TO UNDERTAKE THE MONUMENTAL WORK BY NERO DRUSUS, A ROMAN WARRIOR, WHO HAD DIED 50 YEARS EARLIER

THE **CHURCH OF FOURS** near Tillen, Germany, BUILT BY A MAN WHO INSISTED HE WAS SAVED BY BEING LED FROM THE WILDERNESS BY 4 STAGS, IS AT THE INTERSECTION OF 4 ROADS, IS SHADED BY 4 MAPLES --*AND CAN ACCOMMODATE ONLY 4 WORSHIPERS*

GEORGE WASHINGTON WAS THE ONLY PRESIDENT OF THE UNITED STATES **INAUGURATED IN 2 DIFFERENT CITIES-** *HIS FIRST INAUGURATION TOOK PLACE IN NEW YORK IN APRIL, 1789, AND HIS SECOND IN PHILADELPHIA IN MARCH, 1793*

B not yy ^nor ^nice lest u.c. how A fool u.b.

ADAGE AS WRITTEN BY LORENZO DOW FAMED AMERICAN TRAVELING PREACHER WHICH TRANSLATES: " *Be not too wise nor over nice lest you see how great a fool you be*"

THE **TOMBSTONE** of **THE ORIGINAL MARK TWAIN**

THE GRAVESTONE in St. Louis, Mo., of STEAMBOAT CAPTAIN ISAIAH SELLERS WHO FIRST USED THE NOM DE PLUME MARK TWAIN-- *WHICH WAS ADOPTED BY WRITER SAMUEL CLEMENS TO SHOW HIS ADMIRATION FOR SELLERS* FOR YEARS BEFORE HIS DEATH CAPT. SELLERS CARRIED HIS TOMBSTONE WITH HIM ABOARD HIS SHIP

39

ONE BROTHER WAS BEQUEATHED THE 3 HOUSES AND ANOTHER AN AREA OF THE GROUND THAT HAD TO EQUAL THAT WILLED TO HIS BROTHER

Here's how they divided it ——→

KILLING A BLOODHOUND
IN MEDIEVAL FRANCE WAS A CRIME PUNISHABLE BY A FINE OF 4,500 FRANCS --*EQUIVALENT TODAY TO $86,800*

THE STEEPLE CLOCK
IN THE CHURCH OF ST. NICHOLAS, IN BRISTOL, IS THE ONLY ONE IN ALL ENGLAND *WITH A HAND MARKING THE SECONDS*

ONLY WOMEN
of the Hadjerai Tribe of Chad, Africa,
ARE PERMITTED TO SMOKE PIPES--
THE MEN CAN ONLY CHEW TOBACCO

THE FIRST FINGER PAINTER

CORNELIS KETEL (1548-1616)
THE RENOWNED DUTCH ARTIST
PAINTED WITH EQUAL DEFTNESS
WITH A BRUSH,
HIS FINGERS--OR HIS TOES

THE TREASURY DOOR
of Tewkesbury Abbey, England,
IS REINFORCED WITH
STRIPS OF METAL
*TAKEN FROM THE ARMOR OF
KNIGHTS SLAIN IN THE BATTLE
OF TEWKESBURY IN 1471*

| MR. and MRS. | MR. and MRS. | MR. and MRS. | MR. and MRS. |
| HENRY WALTNER | HENRY MILLER | BEN J. WALTNER | JOHN M. MILLER |

4 COUPLES WHO WERE MARRIED IN A JOINT CEREMONY
IN FREEMAN, SO. DAKOTA, IN 1910
CELEBRATED THEIR 60th WEDDING ANNIVERSARIES TOGETHER (Oct. 6, 1970)

MARSHAL BESSIÈRES
(1768 - 1813)
WAS KILLED FIGHTING FOR
THE FRENCH AGAINST AUSTRIA,
YET HIS WIDOW WAS PAID A
PENSION FOR 25 YEARS BY
THE EMPEROR OF AUSTRIA-
THE EMPEROR GRANTED IT
BECAUSE HER HUSBAND HAD
SHOWN TOLERANCE IN
RULING AUSTRIAN PROVINCES
CONQUERED BY FRANCE

THE MONASTERY of St. CATHERINE
WAS BUILT AT THE FOOT OF MOUNT
SINAI IN 520 ON ORDERS OF
BYZANTINE EMPEROR JUSTIN I
--WHO ORDERED THE ARCHITECT EXECUTED
BECAUSE HE HAD OVERLOOKED THE EASE WITH
WHICH IT COULD BE ATTACKED *BY HURLING
DOWN ROCKS FROM THE MOUNTAINTOP-*
HISTORY RECORDS NO INSTANCE OF
IT EVER HAVING BEEN ATTACKED

THE MOST PATIENT "FISHERMAN"

THE DARTER of Panama

WHICH DIVES IN THE WATER
TO CATCH FISH HAS WINGS
THAT BECOME WATERLOGGED

--SO IT MUST SPREAD THEM OUT
TO DRY AFTER EVERY DIVE

BIRKS' CLOCK in Vancouver, B.C.,

SINCE ITS
INSTALLATION
IN 1902
HAS LOST
ONE MINUTE
EACH SUMMER
*AND GAINED
ONE MINUTE
EACH WINTER*

U.S. SOLDIERS

ON A MARCH THROUGH HEAVY
SNOWDRIFTS IN WYOMING IN 1857
SENT A FEW TROOPERS AHEAD
TO CREATE A FIRMLY PACKED PATH
*BY CRAWLING ON THEIR
HANDS AND KNEES*
THE ADVANCE MEN HAD TO BE
CHANGED EVERY 50 YARDS

**THE SEAMAN WHO COULD NOT
ESCAPE HIS FATE**
ROBERT SIMPSON
AS A 15-YEAR-OLD SHIP'S BOY
WAS ONE OF 4 MEMBERS OF THE
CREW OF THE "LOCH SLOY" SAVED
ON APRIL 24, 1899, WHEN THE SHIP
*WAS WRECKED OFF CAPE BORDA,
AUSTRALIA* -- 6 YEARS LATER THE
"LOCH SLOY'S" SISTER SHIP THE
"LOCH VENNACHAR", WAS WRECKED
IN THE SAME SPOT AND SIMPSON
PERISHED WITH THE ENTIRE CREW

THE CHAPEL OF ST. JACQUES
IN THE GARDEN OF THE
CITY HALL OF ORLEANS, FRANCE,
**ACTUALLY IS ONLY A FAÇADE
MEMORIAL--***THE ORIGINAL EDIFICE
HAVING BEEN DESTROYED IN
THE FRENCH REVOLUTION*

43

THE PALACE
of the Archbishop of Paris, France,
NOW BEING RESTORED, HAS SERVED
DURING THE LAST 400 YEARS AS
*A STABLE, GARAGE, LAUNDRY,
CANNERY, JAM FACTORY, OPTICIAN'S
STORE, WAREHOUSE AND THE SHOP
OF A DEALER IN RABBIT SKINS*

THE DUKE de RICHELIEU
(1696-1788)
A PREMATURE BABY,
HAD TO BE KEPT WRAPPED
IN WOOL FOR THE FIRST
5 MONTHS, BUT HE LIVED
TO BE 92 YEARS OF AGE,
*WAS NEVER SICK,
WON 40 DUELS,
WAS WOUNDED 14 TIMES
AND WAS MARRIED 3 TIMES
--THE LAST TIME AT 84*

INDIAN WOMEN
of Tehuantepec, Mexico,
IN COMMEMORATION OF THE RESCUE OF A
BABY FROM DROWNING IN ANCIENT TIMES
*ALWAYS WEAR A HEADDRESS
MADE FROM A BABY'S FROCK*

CHAETODON CAPISTRATUS
A FISH,
FOOLS PREDATORS
BY DISPLAYING A
LARGE FALSE EYE
ON ITS TAIL

THE TIDE
ALONG THE NORTHERN COAST OF ENGLAND'S CORNWALL RISES AND FALLS MORE THAN 20 FEET, SO *SHIPS IN THE HARBOR ARE LEFT HIGH AND DRY TWICE EACH DAY*

HIS DEATH WAS PRODUCED BY BEING SPURRED IN THE HEAD BY A ROOSTER

EPITAPH ON THE GRAVE OF DAVID CORBIN IN THE OLD SCHOOL BAPTIST CHURCHYARD, near Roxbury, N.Y.

HEAVEN KNOWS WHAT MAN HE MIGHT HAVE BEEN. BUT HE DIED A MOST RARE BOY

Epitaph of F.W. JACKSON ON BURIAL HILL, PLYMOUTH, MASS., WHO DIED IN 1799 AT THE AGE OF ONE

CZAR PAUL I
(1754-1801) of Russia
MADE THE WEARING OF A VEST *A CRIME PUNISHABLE BY DEATH*

HE WAS CONVINCED THAT PRACTICE WAS SO RADICAL *THAT IT WAS THE CHIEF CAUSE OF THE FRENCH REVOLUTION*

KARL COUNT HARRACH
(1761-1829) AN AUSTRIAN DIPLOMAT, STARTED STUDYING MEDICINE AT 29 AND WHEN HE BECAME A PHYSICIAN *PRACTICED FOR 25 YEARS WITHOUT ACCEPTING A PENNY IN FEES*

STEPPING STONES
St. Jean Pied du Port, France, CONSTRUCTED IN 778 SO THE FRENCH HERO, ROLAND, COULD CROSS THE RIVER NIVE TO DEFEAT A HOSTILE ARMY *HAS BEEN CAREFULLY PRESERVED FOR 1,193 YEARS*

THE **PAGAN WALL** in Mont St. Odile, France, 10 FEET HIGH, 5 FEET THICK AND 6 MILES LONG, WAS BUILT BY THE CELTS WITHOUT MORTAR AND WITH ONLY WOODEN CLAMPS GRIPPING ITS HUGE BOULDERS --*YET IT HAS ENDURED FOR 2,200 YEARS*

WARROW TRIBESMEN of Guiana, South America, BECAUSE THEIR VILLAGES ARE UNDERWATER 9 MONTHS OF EACH YEAR, LIVE IN COMMUNITY HOUSES BUILT ON TREE TRUNKS --*AND EXIST ON FISH THEY CATCH WITHOUT LEAVING HOME*

TEMPLE COURT AN OFFICE BUILDING IN CINCINNATI, OHIO, WAS BUILT IN 1869 *AS A CHURCH*

THE **SPIDER MONKEYS** of So. America CROSS RIVERS BY LINKING THEMSELVES *TO FORM A LIVING BRIDGE*

47

LOUIS LURIE of San Francisco, Calif., HAS EATEN LUNCH IN THE SAME RESTAURANT AND ALWAYS AT THE SAME TABLE *EVERY DAY FOR 54 YEARS*

THE **ILLUSTRIOUS DROPOUT**
RANDOLPH S. FOSTER (1820-1903) WHO BECAME PRESIDENT OF NORTHWESTERN UNIVERSITY, IN HIS IMPATIENCE TO BE A PREACHER, *LEFT AUGUSTA COLLEGE, KENTUCKY, AT 17 WITHOUT GRADUATING*

DR. **RALPH B. WILLIAMS** OF JUNEAU, ALASKA, WOUNDED BY 2 THUGS IN SAN FRANCISCO IN MAY, 1968, *IS LIVING NORMALLY WITH 5 BULLETS IN HIS HEAD*

THE **FIRST PAYROLL** CUNEIFORM CLAY TABLETS FOUND IN MESOPOTAMIA LIST THE ALLOWANCES PAID TO 1,197 SLAVES *5,000 YEARS AGO*

**MARSHAL CHRETIEN-LOUIS,
de MONTMORENCY-LUXEMBOURG**
(1675-1746) of France
SENT OUT FORMAL INVITATIONS
TO HIS FUNERAL IN 1729
AND AGAIN IN 1739
--*BUT HAD TO CANCEL THE
INVITATIONS BOTH TIMES*

ELIZABETH ADAMS (1824-1920)
SERVED THE TERRERO FAMILY
OF SOUTHAMPTON, ENGLAND,
AS A GOVERNESS UNTIL HER DEATH
AT THE AGE OF 96—
SHE WAS THEIR GOVERNESS
FOR 65 YEARS

THE **GIANT
TOADSTOOL**
of
AUSTRALIA
(BOLETUS
PORTENTATUS)
WEIGHS
MORE THAN
15 POUNDS
*AND IS AS
LARGE AS A
PIANO STOOL*

BARON von **HAMMER-PURGSTALL**
(1774-1856) of Vienna
WAS A DEVOUT CHRISTIAN,
YET HE BECAME SO ENAMORED
OF THE ARABIC LANGUAGE THAT
*HE TRANSLATED THE PRAYER BOOK
INTO ARABIC AND PERFORMED ALL HIS
DEVOTIONS IN THAT LANGUAGE*

ST. MICHAEL'S CHAIR
IN CHEVY CHASE HALL, ON ST. MICHAEL'S MOUNT, ENGLAND, IS ACTUALLY THE STONE FRAME OF AN ANCIENT BEACON-- BUT LEGEND HAS IT THAT THE WIFE OR HUSBAND WHO SITS IN IT AHEAD OF THEIR SPOUSE *WILL BE THE MASTER FOR LIFE*

THE DYING MAN'S THREAT THAT PROVED PROPHETIC
HONGI HIKA chief of the Maoris DYING FROM A BULLET WOUND ON MARCH 6, 1828, TOLD A RIVAL CHIEFTAIN, WHARE UMU:
"You will not survive me by more than a week "
WHARE UMU WAS SLAIN IN BATTLE BEFORE THE END OF THE WEEK

MATHEMATICAL PYRAMID

$$1 \times 9 + 2 = 11$$
$$12 \times 9 + 3 = 111$$
$$123 \times 9 + 4 = 1111$$
$$1234 \times 9 + 5 = 11111$$
$$12345 \times 9 + 6 = 111111$$
$$123456 \times 9 + 7 = 1111111$$
$$1234567 \times 9 + 8 = 11111111$$
$$12345678 \times 9 + 9 = 111111111$$

THE MOUNTED MARKET
THE UZBEKS of Asiatic Russia CONDUCT THEIR MARKET TRANSACTIONS *WITH ALL SELLERS AND BUYERS ON HORSEBACK*

Wohledlgeborne
Frau Maria Ramsauer
Bergmeisters Hattin
alhier

THE **HEADSTONES** of **HALLSTATT** — THE **SKULL** OF EACH CORPSE IN HALLSTATT, AUSTRIA, IS REMOVED FROM ITS GRAVE AFTER 10 YEARS, BLEACHED AND STORED IN A BONE WAREHOUSE -- *WITH AN IDENTIFYING INSCRIPTION ON IT*

GIRLS in Pakistan CHARM COBRAS *BY SINGING TO THEM*

A **PLAN** TO ENABLE RAILROADS TO REACH THE TOP OF HIGH MOUNTAINS, EVOLVED IN 1859 BY A GERMAN INVENTOR NAMED FRIEDRICH ALBRECHT, CALLED FOR THE USE OF **BALLOONS**

THE MEN WHO NEVER SIT

SAMBURU MEN of Kenya CONSIDERING IT EFFEMINATE TO SIT *REST BY LEANING AGAINST A FORKED STICK STUCK INTO THE GROUND*

A **ROCK** SHAPED LIKE A *WOODEN SHOE*

A FISHERMAN'S COTTAGE in Conway, Wales, BUILT 160 YEARS AGO *IS THE SMALLEST HOUSE IN GREAT BRITAIN*

JOHN-GO-TO-BED-AT-NOON IS A FLOWER THAT *ALWAYS FOLDS ITS PETALS AT MIDDAY*

THE **HOME**
OF BURR CASWELL, IN MASON COUNTY, MICH., *WAS THE COUNTY'S FIRST RESIDENCE OF A WHITE SETTLER, THE FIRST STORE, THE FIRST JAIL AND THE FIRST COURTHOUSE—IT WAS BUILT IN 1847 FROM LUMBER WASHED ASHORE ON THE BEACH OF LAKE MICHIGAN*

THE **MATAVANU VOLCANO** on Victoria Island in the Pacific **WHICH ERUPTED IN 1905 COVERED EVERY FOOT OF LAND WITH LAVA --EXCEPT THE MOUTH OF A CAVE USED AS A MAUSOLEUM FOR A GIRL HELD IN HIGH ESTEEM BY THE NATIVES**

VILLAGE OFFICIALS FRENCH AND SPANISH HAVE MET AT THE BORDER STONE OF ST. MARTIN TO PLEDGE PEACE BY A SPECIAL HANDSHAKE **ANNUALLY FOR 596 YEARS**

AN **ANIMAL TRAINER** IN THE CONGO KNOWN ONLY AS DR. ASCENSO, WHEN BREAKING ZEBRAS TO THE SADDLE **ALWAYS WORE CLOTHING WITH ZEBRA STRIPES**

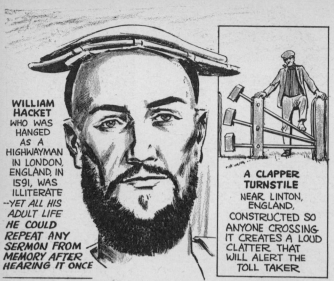

WILLIAM HACKET WHO WAS HANGED AS A HIGHWAYMAN IN LONDON, ENGLAND, IN 1591, WAS ILLITERATE --YET ALL HIS ADULT LIFE *HE COULD REPEAT ANY SERMON FROM MEMORY AFTER HEARING IT ONCE*

A CLAPPER TURNSTILE NEAR LINTON, ENGLAND, CONSTRUCTED SO ANYONE CROSSING IT CREATES A LOUD CLATTER THAT WILL ALERT THE TOLL TAKER

THE **BRISTLEWORM** CAN REPRODUCE BY SPLITTING ITSELF INTO SOME 24 SEGMENTS *EACH OF WHICH GROWS A NEW HEAD AND TAIL*

THE **TRIGGER PLANT** of Australia IS SO SENSITIVE TO ANY TOUCH THAT WHEN A BEE LANDS ON THE FLOWER *THE PLANT SHOOTS ITS POLLEN TOWARD THE INSECT*

LUIS de CAMOENS (1524-1579) of Portugal one of the greatest lyric poets of his time. WAS SO POVERTY STRICKEN IN HIS LATER YEARS THAT HE SUBSISTED ON *FOOD BEGGED FROM PASSERSBY BY A FAITHFUL JAVANESE SERVANT*

KHUDAIAR KHAN
RULER OF KOKAND, IN ASIATIC RUSSIA, WHO HAD CHAFED UNDER THE TUTORSHIP OF A LEGAL GUARDIAN UNTIL HE WAS 18 YEARS OF AGE, AS HIS FIRST OFFICIAL ACT *BEHEADED HIS GUARDIAN AND 600 OF THE LATTER'S FOLLOWERS*

THE **CHAPEL** OF THE CASTLE OF AMBERG, GERMANY, CONSTRUCTED TO LOCATE IT OUTSIDE THE ONE-TIME STATE HOUSE *IS IN A BAY WINDOW*

THE **FLOATING NURSERY** THE GREAT SILVER WATER BEETLE BUILDS A NEST FOR ITS YOUNG BY SPINNING SILKEN THREADS INTO SHEETS WHICH FLOAT BENEATH THE WATER'S SURFACE WITH A TUBE EXTENDING TO THE AIR

JEAN HAMON (1618-1687) FRENCH PHYSICIAN AND PHILAN—THROPIST, SO HE COULD PROVIDE MORE MONEY FOR THE POOR *LIVED FOR 36 YEARS SOLELY ON DOG FOOD*

CHARLES P. FROEBEL
(1788-1824)
A BOOK DEALER IN Rudolstadt, Germany

WITH BOOKS AS HIS ONLY TEACHER *MASTERED 21 LANGUAGES*

THE STAIRWAY TO SECLUSION
THE ENTRANCE TO THE CITY PARK, IN COUTANCES, FRANCE, CONSISTS OF 7 CUP-SHAPED LEVELS SO CONSTRUCTED THAT A PERSON ENTERING OR LEAVING WILL BE *HIDDEN FROM OTHER VISITORS*

THE MOST PATIENT BIRD
THE SILVERY GULL WHICH BREAKS THE SHELLS OF SNAILS AND MUSSELS BY DROPPING THEM FROM GREAT HEIGHTS HAS BEEN OBSERVED REPEATING ITS ATTEMPT TO OPEN A SINGLE SHELL *59 TIMES*

"BILLY"
PARROT PET OF THE LIGHTHOUSE KEEPER AT PORTLAND, MAINE, ALWAYS ANNOUNCED THE FIRST SIGN OF FOG FOR 45 YEARS BY CROAKING: *"JOE, START THE HORN, IT'S FOGGY."*

A POLE
WITH LEAVES IN ITS SPLIT TOP IS ALWAYS STUCK INTO A FIELD PLOWED FOR THE FIRST TIME BY A FARMER OF THE MENDE TRIBE, AFRICA --AND ITS REMOVAL IS *A CRIME PUNISHABLE BY DEATH*

Hallock Castle
THE HOME OF GERARD HALLOCK, in New Haven, Conn., WAS CONSTRUCTED AS A REPLICA OF KENILWORTH CASTLE, ENGLAND, *SUBJECT OF SIR WALTER SCOTT'S FAMOUS "KENILWORTH"*

The Belfry
of St. Thomas Church, in Graz, Austria, OCTAGON SHAPED AND 111 FEET HIGH, WAS ORDERED DEMOLISHED BY NAPOLEON BONAPARTE --BUT HE GOOD-HUMOREDLY RESCINDED HIS ORDER WHEN THE TOWNSPEOPLE OFFERED HIM A BRIBE EQUIVALENT TO $1,200

"Big Ears"
A NATIVE of Mwanza, Tanganyika, WHOSE LOBES WERE SO DISTENDED *HE COULD PASS HIS ARMS THROUGH HIS EARS*

NATIVES of Pinsec, Switzerland, INHABIT THEIR VILLAGE *ONLY 3 MONTHS IN EACH YEAR* EVERYONE IN THE COMMUNITY LIVES IN A VILLAGE HIGH IN THE MOUNTAINS ALL THE REST OF THE YEAR

A PROFILE OF NORWEGIAN EXPLORER ROALD AMUNDSEN CARVED BY NATURE CENTURIES BEFORE HIS BIRTH, IN A CLIFF NEAR NY-ALESUND, NORWAY

GUERIN

A 12-YEAR-OLD FRENCH APPRENTICE CAUGHT ON A GRAPPLING HOOK IN NANTES, FRANCE, ON JULY 16, 1849 *WAS LIFTED TO A HEIGHT OF 2,000 FEET* THE BALLOON CRASHED, YET THE DANGLING BOY ESCAPED UNHARMED

THE **WALLS** of Euryelos Castle, in Syracuse, Sicily
BUILT BY THE ANCIENT GREEKS WITHOUT MORTAR OF ANY KIND
ARE STILL STANDING 2,300 YEARS LATER

CONUS SNAILS
of the Great Barrier Reef,
Australia,
WHEN GRIPPED ANYWHERE
EXCEPT AT THEIR EXTREME
TIP, *ADMINISTER A
POISONOUS STING*

THE **ÆSOP PRAWN**
IS BLUE AT NIGHT
AND IN THE DAYTIME
IS GREEN OR BROWN
-DEPENDING ON THE COLOR
OF THE SEAWEED TO
WHICH IT CLINGS

THE **LARGEST
GOLD NUGGET
IN HISTORY**
THE
HOLTERMANN
NUGGET
MINED ON
HAWKINS' HILL,
New So. Wales,
Australia,
DISCOVERED
ON OCT. 19, 1872,
WAS 4'9"
HIGH,
2'2" WIDE,
AND
WEIGHED
630
POUNDS

THE FIRST IRON WARSHIP

THE "KARTERIA"
A GREEK PADDLE STEAMER COMMANDED
BY CAPTAIN ABNEY HASTINGS, AN
ENGLISHMAN, *WAS THE FIRST
IRON SHIP TO ENGAGE
IN NAVAL WARFARE—*
IT SUCCESSFULLY LED A
GREEK SQUADRON AGAINST
A SUPERIOR TURKISH FLEET
OFF PORT SALONA, GREECE,
ON SEPT. 29, 1826

DIDIER THIRION
(1763-1816)
AS A MEMBER OF THE FRENCH
REVOLUTIONARY ASSEMBLY, VOTED
TO EXECUTE KING LOUIS XVI,
BUT THEN INTRODUCED A LAW
TO ABOLISH THE DEATH
PENALTY SO THE MONARCH
WOULD BE THE LAST FRENCHMAN
SENTENCED TO THE GUILLOTINE

2 SENTRY GEESE
HAVE PATROLLED
THE CLOISTERS OF THE CATHEDRAL
IN BARCELONA, SPAIN, FOR CENTURIES
*IN COMMEMORATION OF THE CAPITOLINE
GEESE OF ROME WHICH SAVED THE
CITY FROM CAPTURE BY THE GAULS*

ELEPHANT ROCK
Bossinney, England
NATURAL ROCK FORMATION

DIMITRIOS TOTSKAS

A HIGHWAYMAN IN GREECE
FROM 1769 TO 1809
DONATED A BAPTISMAL FONT
TO A DIFFERENT CHURCH EACH
YEAR OF THOSE 40 YEARS,
PAID THE ENTIRE COST OF
CONSTRUCTING THE CHURCH
OF AYA PARASKEVI, in Alpokhari,
*AND ENDOWED IT WITH A
FLOUR MILL WHICH ASSURED
IT AN ANNUAL INCOME*

PIETRO FREGOSO

WHO WAS ELECTED RULER OF
GENOA, ITALY, ON JULY 15, 1393,
RESIGNED HIS OFFICE AFTER A
REIGN OF ONLY 2 HOURS

THAT'S
KID
STUFF!

THE
**STEAMER
DUCK**
CAN FLY AS A
FLEDGLING BUT AS
AN ADULT
ONLY WADDLES

61

OUR ATMOSPHERE
IS SHOWERED EVERY 24 HOURS BY
750,000,000,000,000,000
METEORS

EVERY HOUSE
ON THE ISLAND OF ST. STEPHEN, YUGOSLAVIA,
WAS CONSTRUCTED WITH MONEY OBTAINED
BY SELLING THE CARGO OF A
TURKISH WARSHIP WRECKED OFF
THE ISLAND IN THE 15th CENTURY

A **VASE**
CONTAINING THE
BLOOD OF A
MARTYR AND A
SPONGE WAS
FOUND IN THE
WALL OF THE
CATACOMBS
IN ROME.
THE ANCIENTS
BELIEVED A MARTYR'S
BLOOD MADE A WALL
INDESTRUCTIBLE

A **BRIDE** IN 16th CENTURY LAPLAND
ALWAYS WAS MARRIED *WEARING WOOD SKIS*

THE CITY HALL of Altona, Germany, FORMERLY SERVED THE COMMUNITY AS A *RAILROAD STATION*

THE **FIRST AMERICAN PRESIDENT!**

PEDRO de la **GASCA** (1485-1560) SENT FROM SPAIN TO CRUSH A REVOLT IN PERU IN 1546 WAS GIVEN THE TITLE *"PRESIDENT OF THE ROYAL AUDIENCE"*— HE SERVED WITHOUT SALARY --YET WHEN HE RETURNED TO SPAIN 4 YEARS LATER HE CONTRIBUTED $700,000 TO THE SPANISH TREASURY

THE **PUBLIC FOUNTAIN** in Prarolo, Italy, WAS CONSTRUCTED IN 1878 WITH A ROOF TO SHIELD IT FROM THE RAIN SO IT CAN *DOUBLE AS THE BULLETIN BOARD ON WHICH ALL OFFICIAL DECREES ARE POSTED*

THE WISEST FOOL

FREDERICK TAUBMANN (1565-1613) COURT JESTER TO THE RULER OF SAXONY, SERVED AT THE SAME TIME AS *PROFESSOR OF POETRY AT THE UNIVERSITY OF WITTENBERG*

THE WATER LENTIL

DOES ALL ITS GROWING UNDERWATER, RISES FROM THE BOTTOM FOR A SHORT TIME TO POKE ITS BLOSSOMS ABOVE THE SURFACE *-- THEN SINKS BACK INTO THE MUD AND PEAT*

SOME ROADS

in Ladakh, a province in the Himalayas, ARE SO STEEP AND STONY THAT TRAVELERS CAN TRAVERSE THEM ONLY BY CLINGING TO *THE TAIL OF A SPECIALLY TRAINED PONY*

MRS. ELIZABETH A. PRICE of Westbank, British Columbia, WHO WAS BORN ON *JUNE 17th* IS THE MOTHER OF A SON, EDGAR, WHO WAS MARRIED ON *JUNE 17th* AND HAS 2 GRANDCHILDREN GREGG, BORN *JUNE 17th, 1953* AND CAROL, BORN *JUNE 17th, 1955*

MAJOR FREDERICK JACKSON, HAVING EMPTIED HIS RIFLE AT A HUGE BEAR IN FRANZ JOSEF LAND, IN THE ARCTIC, FINALLY DROVE OFF THE ANIMAL *BY THRUSTING THE BARREL INTO ITS MOUTH* (Feb., 1895)

THE **WIVES** OF GARLIC FARMERS OF LAS HURDES, SPAIN, DURING THE HARVEST FESTIVALS *BRAID THEIR HAIR WITH STRINGS OF GARLIC*

THE WITCH'S TREE FOREST OF TRONÇAIS, FRANCE, THE OPENING IN ITS TRUNK *HAS THE NATURAL OUTLINE OF A WITCH*

THE LION and THE SPHINX NATURAL ROCK FORMATION OVERLOOKING KEMPES FJORD, IN NORTHEAST GREENLAND

THE SAFEST BOATMEN IN THE WORLD
THE LARGE ROOFED BOATS OF THE NATIVES OF WAROPEN, PAPUA, *ARE COMPLETELY DISMANTLED AND REASSEMBLED AFTER EACH TRIP*

THE CLAWS OF CALAPPA CRABS ARE AS DIFFERENT AS HUMAN FINGERPRINTS

FLORENCE BROSSART OF NAPLES, FLA. HAS SCORED 8 HOLES-IN-ONE

THE GIANT DRAGON FLY OF NEW ZEALAND, WHICH MEASURES 5 INCHES IN LENGTH, *STEERS ITSELF LIKE AN AIRPLANE BY 2 RUDDERS AT THE TIP OF ITS TAIL*

Mr. and Mrs.
WILLIAM C. HARTMAN
of Baltimore, Maryland,
WERE BOTH BORN IN BALTIMORE,
WERE BOTH BORN ON THE SAME DAY,
AND WERE BOTH BAPTIZED
IN THE SAME CHURCH
ON THE SAME DAY—
MOREOVER, THEIR NAMES APPEAR
ONE DIRECTLY AFTER THE OTHER
IN THE BAPTISMAL RECORD BOOK OF
ST. MICHAEL'S CHURCH of Baltimore

THE
THERAPY PRESCRIBED FOR INMATES OF
THE MENTAL INSTITUTE OF BERLIN, GERMANY,
AND CARRIED OUT FROM 1806 TO 1812
*WAS MILITARY DRILL WITH KNAPSACKS
AND WOODEN GUNS*

THE
LARGEST BALL
OF "STRING" IN
THE WORLD
A BALL OF
BALING TWINE
33 *FEET IN
CIRCUM—
FERENCE*
CONSTRUCTED
OVER A
PERIOD OF
21 YEARS
BY FRANCIS
A. JOHNSON,
OF DARWIN,
MINN.

THE KNAPP TWINS
of Sweden

UNDER SENTENCE OF DEATH, HAD THEIR PUNISHMENT COMMUTED TO LIFE IMPRISONMENT BY KING GUSTAVUS III IN 1778 ON CONDITION ONE WOULD DRINK TEA DAILY AND THE OTHER COFFEE *WHILE SCIENTISTS STUDIED THEIR HEALTH.*

THE MONARCH WAS MURDERED IN 1792, THE 2 PROFESSORS CONDUCTING THE EXPERIMENT BOTH DIED *--AND THE TWINS LIVED TO BE 83 AND 86*

THE CHURCH of SULZBACH-ROSENBERG Germany HAS BEEN SHARED BY PROTESTANTS AND CATHOLICS *FOR 500 YEARS*

THE **FUNNEL FUNGUS** found in Australia LOOKS JUST LIKE A **FUNNEL**

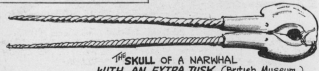

THE **SKULL** OF A NARWHAL *WITH AN EXTRA TUSK* (British Museum)

THE **HATCHET FISH** WHICH LIVES DEEP IN THE OCEAN HAS FIXED EYES THAT CAN ONLY GAZE UPWARD, ROWS OF MAUVE AND VIOLET LIGHTS *AND SKIN THAT IS COMPLETELY TRANSPARENT*

THE **CAPSULES** IN WHICH THE DOG WHELK HATCHES ITS EGGS ARE SHAPED *LIKE FISH*

KILLERS SENT TO THE STRAITS PENAL SETTLEMENT OF PENANG, MALAYA IN THE 19th CENTURY, *WERE BRANDED ON THE FOREHEAD WITH THE WORD "MURDER" IN BOTH ENGLISH AND MALAY*

THE TREE BEDS OF SEMLIKI FOREST, The Congo, Africa, THE SLEEPING COUCHES USED BY NATIVES CONSIST OF A TREE TRUNK WITH 3 BRANCHES--2 OF WHICH SUPPORT THE HEAD OF THE COUCH *AND A THIRD TO SERVE AS THE "PILLOW"*

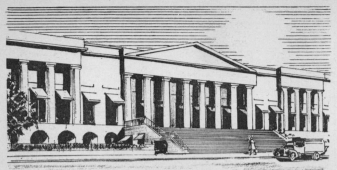

THE **LONGEST STAND IN HISTORY** KHARESHWARI **BABA** of Bombay, India, *HAS STOOD 24 HOURS A DAY FOR 13 YEARS*

HE NEVER SPEAKS, EATS ONLY FRUITS AND VEGETABLES, RESTS ONLY BY LEANING ON A SWING -AND VOWS TO CONTINUE HIS STAND-IN FOR ANOTHER 11 YEARS

THE CITY HALL of Bombay, India, RAISED FUNDS FOR ITS CONSTRUCTION *BY 3 LOTTERIES*

A STONE CROSS NEAR VOLKRATSHOFEN, Germany, ERECTED IN 1458 BY A MURDERER AS *EXPIATION FOR THE SLAYING OF JORG SCHMID AND HIS 4 SONS-* THE KILLER ALSO WAS REQUIRED TO MAKE A PILGRIMAGE TO THE HOLY LAND, RETAIN 20 PRIESTS TO PRAY FOR THE VICTIMS, AND PAY COMPENSATION TO THE WIDOW AND A SURVIVING CHILD

GEORGE HAY FORBES

(1821-1875) ALTHOUGH UNABLE TO USE HIS LOWER LIMBS, BUILT A CHURCH IN Burntisland, Scotland, *UNASSISTED* — ON CRUTCHES HE ALSO SERVED AS SCHOOLTEACHER AND MAYOR OF BURNTISLAND, PRINTED BOOKS AND A MONTHLY MAGAZINE AND TRAVELED EXTENSIVELY THROUGH ITALY, FRANCE AND SPAIN TO COLLECT OLD MANUSCRIPTS

THE MONARCH WHO FOUND THAT NOT EVEN MASS MURDER COULD UPSET A PROPHECY

ROMAN EMPEROR VALENS
(328-378)
TOLD BY A CLAIRVOYANT THAT HIS SUCCESSOR WOULD HAVE A NAME THAT BEGAN WITH THEOD, ROUNDED UP AND EXECUTED HUNDREDS OF PEOPLE ANSWERING THAT DESCRIPTION — *BUT OVERLOOKED ONE MAN* — VALENS WAS SUCCEEDED BY THEODOSIUS, WHO RULED THE EMPIRE FOR 17 YEARS

GIANT WOODEN STATUES IN the CHURCH OF HILDERSHAM, ENGLAND, DEPICTING A CRUSADER AND HIS WIFE *WERE EACH CARVED FROM A SINGLE TREE*

THE ANTARCTIC HAS ACTIVE VOLCANOES AND YOUNG MOUNTAIN RANGES --YET IT IS THE ONLY PART OF THE EARTH *COMPLETELY FREE OF EARTHQUAKES*

MRS. CAROL GREENE of Carthage, Illinois, *HAS MADE 4 HOLES-IN-ONE ON THE SAME 120-YD. SECOND HOLE OF THE CARTHAGE GOLF COURSE*

THE CHURCH of ST. BIAGIO in Finale, Italy, WAS BUILT ADJACENT TO THE CITY WALL 500 YEARS AGO *SO ITS BELFRY COULD REST ON THE WALL—AS A SAVING IN CONSTRUCTION COSTS*

A **HILLTOP CHURCH** IN WEINFELD, IN THE EIFEL SECTOR OF GERMANY, *WAS THE ONLY STRUCTURE THAT SURVIVED WHEN A MYSTERIOUS ENLARGEMENT OF DEAD LAKE ENGULFED EVERY OTHER BUILDING IN THE VILLAGE—* THE CHURCH HAS BEEN CONVERTED INTO A CEMETERY CHAPEL

THE **DOOR TREE** NATURAL FORMATION

Sleeping Giant Park, Hamden, Conn.

THOMAS HALE (1740-1780) AN ENGLISHMAN WHO BECAME A CELEBRATED FRENCH PLAYWRIGHT, NEVER PUT ANYTHING ON PAPER *UNTIL HE HAD PLANNED AN ENTIRE PLAY IN HIS MIND-- PLOT, SCENERY AND EVERY WORD OF DIALOGUE—* HE WOULD THEN WRITE IT FROM MEMORY WITHOUT A SINGLE PAUSE OR CORRECTION

THE **BRAND** of the COFFIN FAMILY'S CATTLE RANCH IN WENATCHEE, WASH., *WAS IN THE SHAPE OF A COFFIN*

THE DYTISCUS BEETLE

FLIES LIKE AN AIRPLANE AND DIVES LIKE A SUBMARINE

IT CLUTCHES A BUBBLE OF AIR AS IT DIVES AND CAN REMAIN UNDERWATER FOR 36 HOURS-- THE BUBBLE SERVING AS A PUMP PRIMER THAT ENABLES IT TO DRAW OXYGEN FROM THE WATER

THE ORATOR WHO WAS CARRIED AWAY BY HIS OWN ELOQUENCE

HATERIUS (63 B.C.-26 A.D.) THE ROMAN SENATOR, REGULARLY BECAME SO MESMERIZED BY HIS OWN ORATORY THAT A SPECIAL AIDE WAS ALWAYS AT HIS SIDE *TO REMIND HIM TO BREATHE*

ELEPHANT FIGHTS in India

ARE STAGED WITH A LOW WALL SEPARATING THE COMBATANTS *SO THEY CANNOT FATALLY INJURE EACH OTHER*

MERKENSTEIN CASTLE in Austria BEARS A NAME THAT MEANS *"REMEMBER THE STONE"* BECAUSE WHEN THE ORIGINAL CASTLE WAS BESIEGED BY TURKS IN 1529 ITS OWNER BURIED ITS TREASURE UNDER A STONE--BUT HER SON, THE ONLY SURVIVOR, WAS *NEVER ABLE TO LOCATE THE RIGHT ROCK*

THE **COCONUT CRAB** OF THE INDIAN AND PACIFIC OCEANS, WHICH IS **3** FEET LONG AND WEIGHS **6** POUNDS, CLIMBS TREES, HURLS COCONUTS TO THE GROUND *AND CAN OPEN CRACKED ONES WITH ITS POWERFUL CLAWS*

THE **RUGGED PATH OF TRUE LOVE** EWART **GROGAN** TO PROVE HIS LOVE FOR GERTRUDE WATT, OF NAPIER, N.Z., MADE THE FIRST TREK FROM THE CAPE OF GOOD HOPE TO THE NORTHERNMOST TIP OF AFRICA *- CROSSING 8000 MILES OF JUNGLE IN A TRIP THAT TOOK 2½ YEARS* HE MARRIED THE GIRL (1897-1900)

FISH ISLAND IN LAKE MAGGIORE, ITALY, IS SO NAMED BECAUSE IT IS *SHAPED LIKE A HUGE FISH*

A SHORT COUNT

ANTOINE de FOURCROY (1755-1809) NOTED FRENCH CHEMIST AND PHYSICIAN WAS MADE A COUNT AT THE AGE OF 54 **3 MINUTES BEFORE HIS DEATH**

DR. I.H. ALEXANDER OF PITTSBURGH, PA., FISHING IN LAKE TIMAGAMI, CANADA, WAS SUDDENLY STARTLED BY A BEAR THAT *CLIMBED INTO HIS ROWBOAT*

DR. ALEXANDER COULDN'T SWIM, SO HE ROWED THE BOAT-- AND BEAR -- TO SHORE

THE **PERIPATUS** STUNS INSECTS BY *SQUIRTING JETS OF MUD*

THE CARPET SHARK LIES MOTIONLESS AT THE BOTTOM OF THE SEA UNTIL SMALL ANIMALS IN SEARCH OF FOOD *ATTEMPT TO NIBBLE ON ITS LEAF-LIKE PROJECTIONS*

THE **FERRY** OVER THE ELILA RIVER, IN THE CONGO, *ACTUALLY CONSISTS OF 4 BOATS LASHED TOGETHER WITH A COMMON PLATFORM* EACH BOAT HAS ITS OWN OARSMAN

76

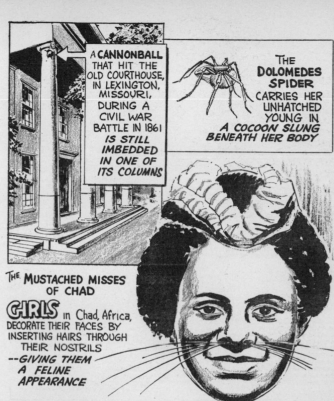

A **CANNONBALL** THAT HIT THE OLD COURTHOUSE, IN LEXINGTON, MISSOURI, DURING A CIVIL WAR BATTLE IN 1861 *IS STILL IMBEDDED IN ONE OF ITS COLUMNS*

THE **DOLOMEDES SPIDER** CARRIES HER UNHATCHED YOUNG IN *A COCOON SLUNG BENEATH HER BODY*

THE **MUSTACHED MISSES** OF CHAD

GIRLS in Chad, Africa, DECORATE THEIR FACES BY INSERTING HAIRS THROUGH THEIR NOSTRILS

--GIVING THEM A FELINE APPEARANCE

CHESS McCARTNEY, of What Cheer, Iowa, ACCOMPANIED BY HIS WIFE AND SON TRAVELED FOR THOUSANDS OF MILES AROUND THE UNITED STATES *IN 2 CARTS PULLED BY TEAMS OF GOATS*

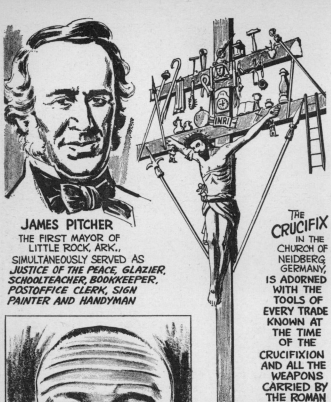

JAMES PITCHER
THE FIRST MAYOR OF LITTLE ROCK, ARK., SIMULTANEOUSLY SERVED AS *JUSTICE OF THE PEACE, GLAZIER, SCHOOLTEACHER, BOOKKEEPER, POSTOFFICE CLERK, SIGN PAINTER AND HANDYMAN*

THE **CRUCIFIX** IN THE CHURCH OF NEIDBERG GERMANY, IS ADORNED WITH THE TOOLS OF EVERY TRADE KNOWN AT THE TIME OF THE **CRUCIFIXION** AND ALL THE WEAPONS CARRIED BY THE ROMAN GUARD

SHILLUK TRIBESMEN of Africa
CAN BE IDENTIFIED BY STRINGS OF WELTS ACROSS THEIR FOREHEAD
--CREATED AT THE AGE OF 14 BY RIPPING THE SKIN WITH A SPECIALLY TREATED FISHBONE

THE **DEEP-SEA BRITTLE STAR** WALKS ON THE MUDDY BOTTOM OF THE OCEAN ON 4 TREMENDOUS LIMBS *EACH 8 TIMES THE LENGTH OF ITS BODY*

John L. DURRANT of Portland, Michigan, AT THE AGE OF 15, PLAYING GOLF AT THE PORTLAND COUNTRY CLUB *SCORED 2 HOLES-IN-ONE ON THE SAME HOLE ON SUCCESSIVE DAYS*

THE **TEMPLE OF THE ELEMENTS** IN PEKING, CHINA, HAS BEEN CONSTRUCTED SO THAT ITS INTERIOR IS OPEN TO THE RAIN, WIND, AND HAIL *--IN THE BELIEF THIS WILL APPEASE THE ELEMENTS*

THE **GATEWAY TO DEATH!** THE CITY GATE of YUN-NAN-FU, CHINA, HAD A CENTRAL ARCH RESERVED FOR THE EMPEROR AND ANYONE ELSE USING IT WAS DECAPITATED *--A MEANS USED BY MANY SUICIDES*

THE FENCE

OUTSIDE THE HOME OF OWEN ALBRIGHT, IN ST. PETERSBURG, FLA., WAS CONSTRUCTED ENTIRELY *FROM HUNDREDS OF THOUSANDS OF SHELLS HE GATHERED ON THE BEACHES OF THE GULF OF MEXICO*

THE MALE BLACK-HEADED GULL

SITS ON THE EGGS TO HATCH THEM AND REFUSES TO ALLOW EVEN ITS MATE TO APPROACH UNTIL SHE MODESTLY TURNS HER HEAD TO THE SIDE -- *THUS IDENTIFYING HERSELF AS A FEMALE*

THE WETA

A WINGLESS NEW ZEALAND CRICKET *HAS ITS EARS IN ITS FRONT LEGS*

ATRANI

A VILLAGE OF 2,600 IN ITALY, CONSISTING OF HOUSES JAMMED TOGETHER BETWEEN A ROCKY MOUNTAIN AND THE SEA, *DOES NOT HAVE A SINGLE STREET TRAVERSING IT*

THE TEMPLE THAT WAS BUILT BY A BEGGAR

THE TEMPLE OF MAHABALESHWAR, in India,
WAS IN RUINS WHEN IT WAS FIRST VIEWED BY A PASSING BEGGAR,
PARSHRAM NARAYAN ANGAL, WHO VOWED THAT HE WOULD SOME DAY
RESTORE IT--*HE FOUND A LOST TREASURE, BECAME A WEALTHY
BANKER, AND KEPT HIS PLEDGE TO RESTORE THE TEMPLE*

The **SHELL** of the Tridacna clam
MEASURING 5 FEET IN LENGTH
IS USED BY CHILDREN ON THE
MOLUCCAS ARCHIPELAGO
AS A BATHTUB

from an
old print

THE **DOWRY** KING HENRY IV OF FRANCE RECEIVED UPON HIS
MARRIAGE TO MARIE DE MÉDICI IN 1600 COMPRISED THE
EQUIVALENT TODAY OF $300,000,000--
BECAUSE HIS ORIGINAL DEMAND FOR THE EQUIVALENT OF ¾ OF A BILLION
DOLLARS WAS REFUSED HE ALSO RECEIVED AS A CONSOLATION
2 TRAINED ELEPHANTS

THE GATE WITH A CHARMED LIFE
THE ALL SAINTS CITY GATE
of Frankfurt-on-the-Main, Germany,
WAS TO HAVE BEEN DEMOLISHED
IN 1807, BUT A MERCHANT
PRESERVED IT BY
CONVERTING IT INTO A
3-STORY BUILDING
IN WORLD WAR II AN
AMERICAN BOMB DESTROYED
THE UPPER TWO STORIES
--BUT THE ORIGINAL GATE
STRUCTURE ESCAPED UNHARMED

THE RIVER THAT WAS
CONDEMNED FOR TREASON!
THE JAIK RIVER
Russia
ACCUSED OF PERMITTING A
REBEL TO CROSS IT, WAS ORDERED
TO STAND TRIAL BY EMPRESS
CATHERINE THE GREAT
AND CONDEMNED TO DEATH!
THE SENTENCE WAS CARRIED OUT
BY RENAMING IT THE
URAL RIVER (1775)

THE REV. GERMAIN GADENNE
(1808-1913) WAS PARISH PRIEST
OF Raches, France,
FOR 80 YEARS
HE PERFORMED ALL HIS
RELIGIOUS FUNCTIONS UNTIL
THE DAY OF HIS DEATH
--AT THE AGE OF **105**

A WHALE'S MOUTH
PROVIDES ENOUGH
WHALEBONE TO MAKE
10,000 BROOMS

A HUGE WALL

THAT STOOD FOR YEARS BESIDE A RAILROAD STATION IN SASKATCHEWAN, CAN., *WAS CONSTRUCTED OF THE SKULLS AND BONES OF MORE THAN 25,000 BUFFALO*

WILD GARLIC
IN THE MIDDLE AGES WAS WORN ON CLOTHING TO *WARD OFF BULLETS*

JEAN THIERRY
(1669-1739)
ACHIEVED FAME AS A RIGHT-HANDED SCULPTOR IN FRANCE, WORKED LEFT-HANDED IN SPAIN AS THE ROYAL SCULPTOR TO KING PHILIP V FOR 7 YEARS -*THEN AGAIN BECAME A RIGHT-HANDED SCULPTOR WHEN HE RETURNED TO FRANCE*

HAUABABA
A VILLAGE NEAR PORT MORESBY, New Guinea, WAS BUILT ON WOOD PILES OVER THE WATER -*TO PROTECT ITS INHABITANTS FROM LAND DEMONS*

HENRY HARRIS
DIED 1837 AGED 15
KILLED BY THE KICK
OF A COLT
WENT TO A WORLD WHERE
HORSES DON'T KICK

EPITAPH in Ross Park Cemetery in Williamsport, Pa.

THE CHURCH of ST. NICHOLAS in Blois, France, WAS BUILT IN 1205 FOR THE EQUIVALENT TODAY OF $360,000 --*RAISED BY THE PEOPLE OF BLOIS SELLING THEMSELVES INTO SLAVERY TO THE CITY OF FOIX FOR 10 YEARS*

KING GEORGE V (1819-1878) WHO RULED HANNOVER, GERMANY, FROM 1851 TO 1866, REVIEWED HIS TROOPS DAILY THROUGHOUT HIS REIGN ALTHOUGH *HE WAS TOTALLY BLIND*

THE WATER STICK INSECT
DINES ON SMALL FISH WHICH IT
CAPTURES WHILE HIDING IN
VEGETATION BENEATH THE SURFACE
*-BREATHING THROUGH AN AIR TUBE
IT STICKS OUT OF THE WATER*

DINKA TRIBESMEN
of the Sudan, Africa,
ALWAYS KNOCK OUT THE
LOWER INCISOR TEETH
OF THEIR SONS BECAUSE
*THE CATTLE WHICH ARE
THEIR LIVELIHOOD HAVE
NO LOWER INCISOR TEETH*

THE MOST AMAZING RECRUITING FEAT IN HISTORY
MAJOR GERSHOM BEACH, DISPATCHED FROM CASTLETON, VT. TO
ENLIST VOLUNTEERS FOR AN ATTACK BY THE GREEN MOUNTAIN BOYS
ON BRITISH FORTS, **WALKED 60 MILES IN 24 HOURS**
AND HE TOOK TIME TO RECRUIT MEN IN RUTLAND, PITTSFORD,
BRANDON, MIDDLEBURY, WHITNEY AND SHOREHAM

A JURY

IMPANELED IN SUSSEX COUNTY, ENGLAND, IN THE 17th CENTURY HAD TALESMEN WITH THE FOLLOWING GIVEN NAMES: *ACCEPTED, REDEEMED, KILL SIN, FAINT NOT, MAKE PEACE, CALLED, GOD REWARD, STANDFAST ON HIGH, EARTH, FLY DEBATE, BE FAITHFUL, RETURN, MORE FRUIT, HOPE FOR, FIGHT THE GOOD FIGHT OF FAITH, GRACEFUL, WEEP NOT AND MEEK*

HANDABE TIABA

A MEMBER OF THE HOUSE OF ASSEMBLY THAT RULES NEW GUINEA, CAN ONLY SPEAK HIS OWN NATIVE DIALECT -- *SO HE CAN NEITHER UNDERSTAND NOR MAKE HIMSELF UNDERSTOOD IN COUNCIL SESSIONS*

THE MEASURING WORM

GUARDS AGAINST PREDATORS *BY LOOKING EXACTLY LIKE A TWIG*

THE WEATHERFISH

GULPS IN HUGE QUANTITIES OF SAND AND DIRT-- *SWALLOWS ANYTHING EDIBLE AND EJECTS THE SAND AND DIRT THROUGH ITS GILLS*

THE PROPHETIC DREAM

MORITZ von ARNDT
(1769-1860)
THE GERMAN POET REPORTED TO HIS PUBLISHER IN 1836 THAT HE HAD SEEN IN A DREAM HIS OWN GRAVESTONE, WITH THE NOTATION *"DIED IN HIS 91st YEAR"* TWENTY-FOUR YEARS LATER HE DIED IN HIS 91st YEAR

MARY HEMENWAY
(1820-1894)
IN 1876 SAVED BOSTON'S HISTORIC OLD SOUTH CHURCH FROM DEMOLITION BY A CASH DONATION FROM HER POCKETBOOK *OF $100,000*

THE TIGER SHARK
IN A SINGLE BIRTH *HAS AS MANY AS 60 LIVE YOUNG*

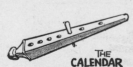

THE CALENDAR
USED BY WAROPEN TRIBESMEN OF PAPUA TO KEEP TRACK OF THE DAYS OF THE WEEK *IS A STICK WITH 7 HOLES --AND A PEG THAT IS MOVED EACH DAY*

The **TIDE** IN THE HARBOR of the island of Sein, France, EMPTIES IT COMPLETELY TWICE EACH DAY --*LEAVING SHIPS STRANDED ON THE MUDDY BOTTOM*

LUCAS GASSEL (1500-1570) of Brussels, Belgium, WAS ONE OF THE MOST CELEBRATED PAINTERS OF HIS TIME --*YET HE NEVER SOLD A SINGLE PAINTING--* INDEPENDENTLY WEALTHY, HE GAVE HIS CREATIONS TO FRIENDS

A **LARGE PEARL** SOLD TO EMPRESS EUGENIE of France FOR $25,000 *WAS FOUND 110 YEARS AGO IN NEW JERSEY*

The **LADY** of **THE LAKE** at Cave Rock. Lake Tahoe, Nev, NATURAL STONE FORMATION

SAMUEL S. LAWS
(1824-1921)
WHO INVENTED THE STOCK TICKER HELD DOCTORATES IN THEOLOGY, SCIENCE, LAW AND MEDICINE AND SERVED AS PRESIDENT OF TWO MISSOURI UNIVERSITIES -WESTMINSTER COLLEGE AND THE UNIVERSITY OF MISSOURI

CORPSES
IN TIMOR, INDONESIA WHILE AWAITING BURIAL ARE *WRAPPED IN BUNDLES AND HUNG IN TREE HOUSES*

THE POCKET-IN-ONE SHOT
J.J. DURAN, PLAYING GOLF AT LOS AMIGOS, IN DOWNEY, CALIF., TEED OFF ON THE 145-YD. THIRD HOLE AND HIS BALL LANDED ON THE GREEN-- *IN THE HIP POCKET OF GREENSKEEPER REUBEN Z. MARES*
Drawn by Reuben Z. MARES, LOS ANGELES, CALIF.

THE GRAVE MARKER OF A KONSO TRIBESMAN OF ETHIOPIA CONSISTS OF A STATUE OF THE DECEASED SURROUNDED BY LIKENESSES *OF ALL THE ENEMIES HE HAS SLAIN*

89

Countess TOROK

HUNGARIAN WIFE OF ABBAS HILMI, WHO RULED EGYPT FROM 1892 TO 1914, BECAUSE OF HER HUSBAND'S INTENSE JEALOUSY *WAS REQUIRED TO WEAR MEN'S CLOTHING WHENEVER SHE LEFT THE PALACE*

THE **GATEWAY** TO JAWBONE WALK, IN EDINBURGH, SCOTLAND, *IS FORMED BY THE JAWBONES OF WHALES*

THE ROCK CHAPEL in Mont St. Odile, France, GOAL OF MANY PILGRIMAGES, WAS MOVED TO ITS PRESENT SITE FROM PARIS --*WHERE IT WAS CONSTRUCTED IN 1925 FOR THE PARIS EXHIBITION OF DECORATIVE ARTS*

JAPANESE SNAILS BEAR FULLY DEVELOPED LIVE OFFSPRING --CAPABLE OF CARING FOR THEMSELVES *WHILE NO LARGER THAN A PEA*

THE CHAPEL OF ST. JOHN in Montigny, Belgium, IS VISITED BY PILGRIMS WHO BELIEVE THEIR VISIT WILL *CURE THEIR CHILDREN OF A FEAR OF THE DARK*

THE MONARCH WHO COULDN'T SQUANDER ALL HIS MONEY

KING PTOLEMY PHILADELPHUS (309-247 B.C.) of Egypt WAS NOTORIOUS FOR HIS WILD EXTRAVAGANCES --YET HE LEFT A FORTUNE EQUAL IN PURCHASING POWER TODAY OF *$88,000,000,000*

THE BELFRY OF THE CHURCH OF RÜNGSDORF, GERMANY, HAS BEEN STANDING FOR 840 YEARS -*HAVING OUTLASTED 3 CHURCHES*

LEPTON CLAMS CAN SURVIVE ONLY BY *ATTACHING THEMSELVES TO THE BOTTOM OF A CRAYFISH*

THE BRIDGE SUPPORTED BY TWIGS
A BRIDGE 100 FEET LONG OVER THE RIVER CHANDRA, IN LADAKH, IN THE HIMALAYAS, IS CONSTRUCTED ENTIRELY OF BIRCH POLES *TIED TOGETHER WITH BIRCH TWIGS*

MRS. TOM HENRY
of Athens, Ohio, HAS FOUND
A 10-LEAF CLOVER
A 9-LEAF CLOVER
TWO 8-LEAF CLOVERS
SIX 7-LEAF CLOVERS
SIXTY-FIVE 6-LEAF CLOVERS
EIGHT 5-LEAF CLOVERS
AND 27,370 *4-LEAF CLOVERS*

THE MOTH THAT WEARS A MASK
THE PUSS MOTH, TO FRIGHTEN AWAY PREDATORS INFLATES A FOLD OF SKIN THAT *BECOMES A SCOWLING, RED FALSE FACE*

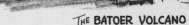

THE BATOER VOLCANO
ON THE ISLAND OF BALI, ERUPTING IN 1905 EMITTED A STREAM OF LAVA THAT THREATENED TO ENGULF THE VILLAGE OF BAROET--*BUT THE LAVA STOPPED AT THE WALL OF THE VILLAGE TEMPLE -- AGAINST WHICH IT STILL RESTS*

MRS. **CATHERINE SALERNO**
OF WHITTIER, CALIF.,
AT THE AGE OF **76**
HAS PERFECT TEETH
--*WITHOUT A SINGLE CAVITY*

NOBLE-BORN YOUNG LADIES
IN 19TH CENTURY CHINA
PRACTICED UNTIL THEY COULD
WRITE THE CHINESE CHARACTERS
FOR "PERSEVERANCE IN LOVE"
*BY SQUIRTING A BLACK STAIN
ON A SCREEN FROM THEIR MOUTHS*

INSECT WITH A FUR COAT
THE LARVA OF THE
COLEOPHORO MOTH
DRESSES ITSELF IN
BITS OF FURRY
LEAVES--WHICH
IT GLUES TOGETHER

KING CHARLES IV
(1748-1819) of Spain
ALWAYS CARRIED 6 WATCHES
EACH INDICATING A DIFFERENT TIME

HOW TO DUPLICATE THE KNIGHT'S
HELMET BY CUTTING OUT AND
REASSEMBLING THE NUMBERED
PARTS OF THE RECTANGLE !

Solution

93

FISHHOOK USED BY **ESKIMOS** of Alaska IS ADORNED WITH THE CARVED HEAD OF A WIZARD *TO ASSURE A BOUNTIFUL CATCH*

The **WOLF GIRL** Kamala, a Hindu girl WAS ADOPTED, FED AND REARED BY A FEMALE WOLF IN 1912--AND WHEN RESCUED 8 YEARS LATER *COULD ONLY WALK ON ALL FOURS AND HOWL* SHE WAS FINALLY TAUGHT TO WALK UPRIGHT, SPEAK AND EAT LIKE A HUMAN AT AN ORPHANAGE IN MIDNAPORE (India)

JEAN-FRANÇOIS CHAMPOLLION (1790-1832) THE FATHER OF EGYPTOLOGY AND FIRST MAN TO DECIPHER EGYPTIAN HIEROGLYPHICS, *WAS A COLLEGE PROFESSOR AT THE AGE OF 18*

THE **BODY** OF KING HENRY IV, of France, EXHUMED FROM ITS GRAVE IN THE CHURCH OF ST. DENIS IN 1793, WAS FOUND TO BE PERFECTLY PRESERVED *ALTHOUGH HE HAD BEEN DEAD FOR 183 YEARS* — THE BODY OF EVERY OTHER FRENCH MONARCH EXHUMED AT THE SAME TIME HAD BEEN REDUCED TO A SKELETON

HAD ARMS SO LONG THAT HE COULD TIE THE GARTERS OF HIS HIGHLAND HOSE 2 INCHES BELOW THE KNEE *WITHOUT STOOPING*

A FAUCET
IN THE KRISHNA TEMPLE, IN MAHABALESHWAR, INDIA, PRODUCES WATER 5 TIMES AS HOLY AS ANY INDIAN STREAM *BECAUSE ITS WATER FLOWS FROM 5 HOLY RIVERS --THE KISTNA, VENNA, KOYANA, CAYATRI AND SAWITRA*

AMPHIOXUS
A FISH
LAYS ITS EGGS AT SUNSET *--AND THEY HATCH BEFORE THE NEXT DAWN*

THE SINGING SANDS OF THE GOBI DESERT
WIND, BLOWING OVER THE SAND DUNES, CAUSES A CONSTANT SOUND THAT VARIES **FROM A ROLL OF DRUMS TO A DEEP CHANT**

THE GIANT GREEN TURTLE

WEIGHING 300 POUNDS IS A DELICACY NATIVES OF PUKA PUKA, ON THE TUAMOTU ARCHIPELAGO, CONSUME FROM *THE TIP OF ITS NOSE TO ITS FEET AND TAIL -- INCLUDING THE SHELL !*

THE MAN WHO WAS KILLED FOR CLAPPING HIS HANDS

JOSEPH-FRANÇOIS FOULLON (1715-1789) FRENCH ADMINISTRATOR WHO WAS SEIZED BY A REVOLUTIONARY MOB, WAS ABOUT TO BE HANGED WHEN HE WAS SAVED BY GENERAL LAFAYETTE *--WHO WAS SO POPULAR THE CROWD APPLAUDED HIM--* BUT WHEN FOULLON JOINED IN THE APPLAUSE HIS ACTION ENRAGED THE MOB *WHICH SEIZED HIM AGAIN AND HANGED HIM FROM A LAMPPOST*

THE AMAZON BASIN LUNGFISH

MUST STAND ON ITS TAIL TO BREATHE ABOVE WATER *--OR IT WILL DROWN*

JAMES H. FAIRCHILD (1817-1902) WAS CONNECTED WITH OBERLIN COLLEGE, OHIO, AS A STUDENT, TUTOR, PROFESSOR, PRESIDENT AND ACTIVE PROFESSOR EMERITUS *CONTINUOUSLY FOR 68 YEARS*

THE **BATTLE** of **MONTLERI** France FOUGHT ON JULY 16, 1465 *ENDED WITH BOTH ARMIES FLEEING*

THE DUKE OF BURGUNDY OFFERED TO TOSS A COIN WITH KING LOUIS XI TO DETERMINE A VICTOR --BUT THE MONARCH REFUSED

from an old print

HOW TO REDUCE THIS AREA BY EXACTLY ONE FOURTH

Solution:
DIVIDE THE OUTLINE

3 2 1 4

TO FORM A SQUARE FROM WHICH ONE FOURTH CAN BE REMOVED EASILY

1 3
4
2

THE **SNOWSHOES** USED BY JAPANESE HUNTERS LONG BEFORE ADMIRAL PERRY VISITED THE COUNTRY, WERE PROVIDED WITH LEATHER "REINS" *TO MAKE IT EASIER TO CHANGE DIRECTION*

ANTOINE HASECH (1601-1726) SERVED AS CURATE OF GULLICH, LUXEMBOURG, *FOR 100 YEARS* — HE LIVED TO BE 125

THE **SHWE-DAGON PAGODA** IN RANGOON, BURMA, WHICH IS 370 FT. HIGH, WAS FIRST GILDED IN THE 15th CENTURY BY QUEEN SHIN SAWBU, WHO DONATED HER OWN WEIGHT IN GOLD--101 POUNDS

THE **SMALLEST DULCIMER IN THE WORLD**
BILL DAVIS of Gatlinburg, Tenn., HAS MADE AND PLAYS A PERFECTLY TUNED DULCIMER THAT IS *ONLY 5½ INCHES LONG AND WEIGHS ½ AN OUNCE* —A STANDARD-SIZE DULCIMER, AN ANCIENT STRINGED MUSICAL INSTRUMENT, IS 39" LONG AND WEIGHS 2½ LBS.

THE **NEST** OF THE MASON BEE IS ALWAYS CONSTRUCTED INSIDE A SNAIL SHELL --WHICH IT SEALS CLOSED AND CAMOUFLAGES WITH PINE NEEDLES AND MOSS

ALONSO TOSTADO

(1400-1455) BISHOP OF AVILA, SPAIN, WROTE A BOOK EACH WEEK FOR 35 YEARS
--*A TOTAL OF 1,820 BOOKS*

THE TREE WITH A HEART OF STONE

AN IPABOY TREE in San Ignacio, Argentina, *THAT HAS COMPLETELY ENVELOPED A STONE COLUMN 7 FEET HIGH PART OF A CHURCH RUIN*

THE HOTELS THAT COLLIDED ON A HIGHWAY

THE SPRINGWATER HOTEL, A 3-STORY STRUCTURE IN WENATCHEE, WASH., WASHED OFF ITS FOUNDATION BY A FLASH FLOOD, *CROSSED A 60-FOOT-WIDE HIGHWAY AND COLLIDED WITH THE TERMINAL HOTEL* (Sept.5, 1925)

PICTURE OF A DEER

in the Buckhorn Museum, in San Antonio, Texas, *CREATED FROM THE RATTLES OF 637 RATTLESNAKES*

RUTH WALL of Durhamville, N.Y., MADE A HOLE-IN-ONE *IN HER FIRST ROUND OF GOLF*

A **STONE NEST** CONTAINING PERFECTLY FORMED STONE EGGS *CREATED BY NATURE* Moeraki Beach, Otago, N.Z.

THE **SIGM SHRINE** IN KASHGAR, CHINESE TURKESTAN, IS BELIEVED TO HAVE THE POWER TO HEAL SKIN AILMENTS *IF A HANDFUL OF MUD IS FLUNG AT A WALL OF THE SHRINE*

THE **ROWBOATS** USED BY THE FISHERMEN OF AVEIRO, PORTUGAL, ARE 50 FEET LONG, WEIGH 15 TONS AND HAVE OARS MEASURING 33 FEET--*EACH OF WHICH IS PULLED AND PUSHED BY 8 ROWERS*

NY-ALESUND

IN NORWAY'S FAR NORTH, ON THE ARCTIC OCEAN, HAS THE *MOST NORTHERN RAILROAD STATION IN THE WORLD*

THE **BAPTISMAL FONT** OF THE CHURCH OF SANTA MARIA, IN BROZAS, SPAIN, *IS THE HOLLOW TOP OF A COLUMN SALVAGED FROM A DEMOLISHED CHURCH*

THE **BEAUTY** WHO BECAME A PUBLIC ATTRACTION BY CITY ORDINANCE *Paule Viguier* (1518-1610) of TOULOUSE, FRANCE, WAS SO BEAUTIFUL THAT WHEN SHE REMAINED INDOORS FOR SEVERAL DAYS *THE POPULACE RIOTED!* THE CITY ADOPTED A LAW REQUIRING HER TO APPEAR ON HER BALCONY TWICE EACH DAY--WHICH SHE DID UNTIL HER DEATH AT THE AGE OF **92**

SNAKES in the mountains of Valais, Switzerland, LIE ON THE SHORES OF MOUNTAIN STREAMS *AND SEIZE TROUT WHEN THEY LEAP ABOVE THE WATER*

A **YOUNG WOMAN** OF THE MUGANDA TRIBE, OF UGANDA, AFRICA, CONSIDERS IT BAD FORM TO CARRY ANYTHING IN HER HANDS -*BALANCING EVEN AN UMBRELLA ON HER HEAD*

THE **IDOL** THAT FANS ITSELF
Koili, India
THE STATUE OF GANESH IN THE TEMPLE OF TARNETAR HAS A BANYAN TREE GROWING FROM ITS RIGHT FOOT -AND WHENEVER A WIND RUSTLES THE LEAVES *THE IDOL APPEARS TO BE WAVING A FAN*

THE LADIES OF MERDANEL
NEAR MONT DAUPHIN, FRANCE
NATURAL STONE SCULPTURE

AUDITEURS DE RADIO
ayez égard à vos voisins

THE CANCELLATION
OF SWISS POSTAGE STAMPS FOR A TIME BORE THE PLEA:
" *RADIO LISTENERS THINK OF YOUR NEIGHBORS* "

A **CARPET FACTORY** in Glasgow, Scotland, BUILT AS A FAITHFUL REPLICA OF *THE DOGE'S PALACE IN VENICE*

DIZU **TRIBESMEN** OF THE GEMIRA PROVINCE OF ETHIOPIA WEAR NO CLOTHING EXCEPT A CAPE MADE BY DRAPING OVER THEIR SHOULDERS A *BUNDLE OF DRIED GRASS*

A **CHIMPANZEE** WAS TRAINED AT YALE UNIVERSITY LABORATORY FOR PRIMATES TO OBTAIN FOOD FROM A VENDING MACHINE *- IN EACH CASE SELECTING THE PROPER TOKEN*

MR. AND MRS. DAVID STEPHENS FISHING AT ERWIN, N.C., HOOKED AN OLD AUTOMOBILE TIRE *CONTAINING 9 CATFISH*

THE BEARDED FLYING FISH HAS 2 LONG WHISKERS *--OFTEN AS LONG AS ITS ENTIRE BODY*

A **TRUCK CHASSIS** near Alderpoint, Calif., *AROUND WHICH A FIR TREE HAS BEEN GROWING FOR 50 YEARS*

CLAUDE JOFRAIN (1639-1721) PREACHED A SERMON EVERY DAY FOR 61 YEARS -- MORE THAN 22,000 *DIFFERENT SERMONS*

THE BEEHUNTER RAPS WITH ITS BEAK ON THE ENTRANCE TO A BEEHIVE--AND WHEN THE *GUARD* BEES EMERGE TO INVESTIGATE, *IT GOBBLES THEM UP*

JUAN BAUTISTA de ANZA (1735-1788) THE FOUNDER OF SAN FRANCISCO LED A FORCE OF 240 SOLDIERS, WOMEN AND CHILDREN OVERLAND FROM SONORA, MEX., TO MONTEREY, CALIF., AND NOT ONLY DID NOT LOSE ANY OF HIS COMPANY *BUT ARRIVED WITH 4 INFANTS BORN ENROUTE* 1775

THE **BELFRY** OF ST. MARK'S CHURCH, IN VENICE, ITALY, 325 FEET HIGH, WHICH CRASHED IN SECONDS ON JULY 14, 1902, *HAD TAKEN 461 YEARS TO CONSTRUCT*

MONGOL HUNTERS TO LURE THE WAPITI DEER INTO RANGE IMITATE ITS CALL BY BLOWING ON *THE BARREL OF A SHOTGUN*

A **COW** OWNED BY BOB CHILDER, A FARMER OF HOLDENVILLE, OKLA., *REGULARLY CAUGHT FISH ON LINES STRUNG AROUND ITS NECK*

SHARK HEADS ARE STILL HUNG FROM POLES CARVED TO RESEMBLE MERMAIDS BY SICILIANS --EXACTLY AS THE PRACTICE WAS ORIGINATED *BY THEIR ANCESTORS, THE HEATHEN SICULS*

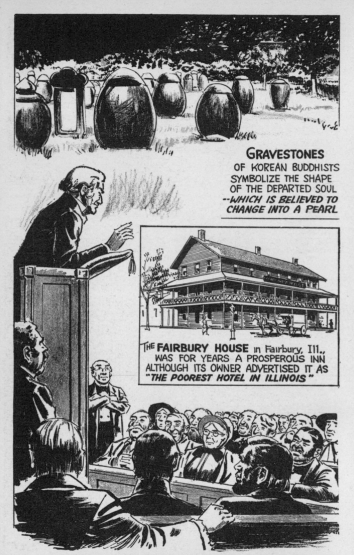

GRAVESTONES OF KOREAN BUDDHISTS SYMBOLIZE THE SHAPE OF THE DEPARTED SOUL *--WHICH IS BELIEVED TO CHANGE INTO A PEARL*

THE **FAIRBURY HOUSE** in Fairbury, Ill., WAS FOR YEARS A PROSPEROUS INN ALTHOUGH ITS OWNER ADVERTISED IT AS *"THE POOREST HOTEL IN ILLINOIS"*

THE **THE PASTOR WHO ALWAYS PADDED HIS CONGREGATION** REV. JOHN PRICE (1803-1887) WHOSE SERMONS in LlanBedr-Paincastle, Wales, WERE POORLY ATTENDED, *HIRED VAGRANTS AT THE EQUIVALENT OF 12 CENTS EACH TO ATTEND HIS SERVICES EACH SUNDAY*

"ROCK" POETRY

JOHANN FRENZEL (1609 -1674) PROFESSOR OF POETRY AT THE UNIVERSITY of LEIPZIG, Germany, COULD ONLY COMPOSE HIS POETRY *WHILE ROLLING ON THE GROUND*

A MESSY ISSUE

MASSIMO BONTEMPELLI and ALBERTO SPAINI BOTH of Milan, Italy, FOUGHT A DUEL IN WHICH BOTH WERE WOUNDED *OVER WHICH TYPE OF SPAGHETTI IS BETTER -- PLAIN OR FLAVORED WITH MEAT SAUCE*

FRESH-WATER CATFISH IN THE TROPICS *CAN CLIMB A HIGH WALL*

STORMS
IN THE DESERTS OF ASIATIC RUSSIA
CREATE GREAT COLUMNS OF SAND
300 FEET HIGH -- *WHICH OFTEN
STAND FOR HOURS*

SANS SOUCI a cottage in
Siasconset, on Nantucket, Mass.,
HAS 13 WINDOWS
NO TWO OF WHICH ARE ALIKE

NATIVES of Whakarewarewa, N.Z.,
COOK ALL THEIR FOOD
IN FIBER BASKETS
LOWERED INTO HOT SPRINGS

THE
TOOTH-
BILLED
PIGEON
OF SAMOA
HAS ITS TEETH
IN ITS BILL

THE **ALEXANDER COLUMN** IN LENINGRAD, RUSSIA, WHICH IS 153½ FEET HIGH, WAS ERECTED IN THE WINTER OF 1834 AND TO KEEP ITS MORTAR FROM FREEZING *IT WAS MIXED WITH HUNDREDS OF BARRELS OF VODKA*

WOMEN
OF THE KONSO TRIBE IN ETHIOPIA AVERAGE A TOTAL OF *EIGHT HUSBANDS*

THE **AFRICAN JABIRU** SLEEPS STANDING UP *WITH THE LONG TOES OF ONE FOOT WRAPPED AROUND THE OPPOSITE KNEE* THIS POSTURE IS IMITATED BY DINKAS AND NUERS TRIBESMEN

THE **SLIME EEL** IS ONLY 18 INCHES LONG BUT TO MAKE ITSELF TOO SLIPPERY FOR CAPTURE, IT CAN EXUDE FROM ITS SKIN ENOUGH LUBRICANT TO FILL *A 2-GALLON BUCKET*

THE **BONTOC IGOROTS** of Luzon, in the Philippine Islands,

PLAY DANCE MUSIC ON BRASS GONGS *THE HANDLES OF WHICH ARE HUMAN JAWBONES*

THE **STICKBAG** AN ALGA, ALWAYS ATTACHES ITSELF TO ANOTHER SEAWEED *- YET IT IS NOT A PARASITE AND GETS ITS NOURISHMENT INDEPENDENTLY*

CAPER

A FLOWERING PLANT THRIVES BEST ON ANCIENT RUINS AND HAS BEEN GROWING ON THE MARBLE COLUMNS OF THE ROMAN COLOSSEUM *FOR 1,500 YEARS*

LES ALDUDES

A VILLAGE ON THE BORDER OF SPAIN AND FRANCE -- SUBJECT OF A BORDER DISPUTE FOR CENTURIES -- WAS FINALLY AWARDED TO FRANCE, BUT AN AREA IN THE CENTER OF THE VILLAGE WILL FOREVER BE *A NO-MAN'S LAND*

THE TRUNK TURTLE
FOUND IN THE MEDITERRANEAN REACHES A LENGTH OF 8 FEET, WEIGHS NEARLY A TON, AND HAS A SHELL SO LARGE THAT NATIVES USE IT *AS A BOAT*

DENNIS SHANNON
INDIANAPOLIS, IND., AT THE AGE OF 13 CAN SIMULTANEOUSLY PALM *2 BASKETBALLS*

THE BALANCING ROCK
Shrewsbury, Mass.
A HUGE BOULDER THAT BALANCES ON A PROJECTION *NO LARGER THAN A MAN'S HAND*

THE TREE FROG
of the W. Indies LIVES IN TREETOPS *AND EVEN LAYS ITS EGGS IN THE BRANCHES OF A TREE*

CHARLES MALINCORNE
A BOOK DEALER OF PARIS, FRANCE, COULD READ ANYTHING EXCEPT *HIS OWN NAME—*
HIS OWN SIGNATURE WHETHER WRITTEN OR PRINTED, WAS INVISIBLE TO HIM

THE **CANCELLATION STAMP** USED BY THE POSTMASTER OF AUGUSTA, MAINE, FROM 1823 TO 1835 *WAS SHAPED LIKE A HORN OF PLENTY*

KASHMIRIS

WHO ARE MOHAMMEDANS *WIND THEIR TURBANS FROM RIGHT TO LEFT*

BUTTON THEIR COATS FROM RIGHT TO LEFT

AND MOUNT THEIR HORSES FROM THE LEFT BUT THOSE WHO ARE HINDUS DO ALL THREE IN THE OPPOSITE MANNER

SIR JOHN COPE

DISMISSED AS BRITISH COMMANDER-IN-CHIEF BECAUSE HE LOST THE BATTLE OF PRESTOPANS TO THE JACOBITE HIGHLANDERS *BET EVERY PENNY OF HIS SAVINGS--$50,000-- THAT HIS SUCCESSOR WOULD ALSO BE DEFEATED BY THE SCOTS--* THE FOLLOWING YEAR GENERAL HENRY HAWLEY, HIS SUCCESSOR, WAS WHIPPED BY THE SCOTS IN THE BATTLE OF FALKIRK

THE GLOBE FISH

WHEN SWIMMING TIRES IT, *FLOATS BY PUFFING ITSELF UP WITH AIR*

A **CASTLE OF COINS**
ON THE BAR OF A HOTEL
IN WHANGAREI, N.Z.,
COLLECTING PENNIES AND OTHER
COINS FOR HANDICAPPED CHILDREN
YIELDED $29,000

THE "CLINTS"
OF YORKSHIRE, ENGLAND,
ARE FIELDS COVERED
WITH HUGE BOULDERS
*--SHAPED LIKE A
GIANT'S MOLARS*

KING MAX JOSEPH
(1756-1825) of Bavaria
IGNORED HIS BIRTHDAY AND
CELEBRATED INSTEAD THE DAY
OF HIS PATRON SAINT, MAXIMILIAN
-- OCTOBER 12TH

BUT IN THE LAST 6 YEARS OF HIS
LIFE THERE WAS NO FETE BECAUSE:

*OCT. 12, 1820 A FIRE DESTROYED
THE ROYAL PALACE*

*OCT. 12, 1821 HIS FAVORITE
SERVANT DIED*

*OCT. 12, 1822 ONE OF HIS
CABINET MINISTERS LOST A
HAND IN AN EXPLOSION*

*OCT. 12, 1823 THE QUEEN SUFFERED
A SEVERE HEMORRHAGE*

*OCT. 12, 1824 SEVERAL WORKMEN
WERE KILLED WHEN A
PALACE WALL COLLAPSED*

OCT. 12, 1825 THE KING DIED !

A DIVING BELL
SUSPENDED BETWEEN 2 SMALL
BOATS WAS USED TO HUNT
SUNKEN TREASURE OFF SPAIN
IN **1678**

THE DEBRIS
OF THE WHITE BARNARD GLACIER of Alaska
*DISPLAYS ALL THE COLORS OF THE TRIBUTARIES
OUT OF WHICH THE GLACIER WAS FORMED*

A **HUGE EAGLE**
SNATCHED UP AN 8-YEAR-OLD
BOY, JEMMIE KENNEY, IN
TIPPAH COUNTY, MISS., IN 1868,
*CARRIED HIM ALOFT—AND THEN
DROPPED HIM TO HIS DEATH*

THE **COLONIAL
SEA SQUIRT**
ACTUALLY CONSISTS OF
A NUMBER OF INDIVIDUAL
ANIMALS JOINED BY A
COMMON BASE BY WHICH
THEY MOVE ABOUT
IN UNISON

THE **UNFINISHED TOWER**
of Leeuwarden, Holland, ON WHICH
CONSTRUCTION WAS STARTED IN
1529, WAS TO BE PART OF A CHURCH
WHICH WAS NEVER BUILT—
*WHEN IT REACHED A HEIGHT
OF 98 FEET IT WAS FOUND
TO BE 56 INCHES OFF CENTER
-- AND IT HAS BEEN A
CURIOSITY FOR 438 YEARS*

A GLASS **THERMOMETER** MADE IN FLORENCE, ITALY, IN 1657 IS DIVIDED INTO *420 DEGREES*— IT USES ALCOHOL INSTEAD OF MERCURY

AISSAOUA BUCHAIB
of Morocco

CAN LET A DEADLY ADDER BITE HIM IN THE FOREHEAD *WITHOUT ILL EFFECTS*— HE COMPRESSES THE VEINS IN HIS NECK SO THAT THE BLOOD FLOWS FREELY AND WASHES THE POISON FROM HIS WOUND

THE **CHURCH OF ST. SAVIOR** ON THE ISLAND OF YEU, FRANCE, WAS BUILT AROUND A LIGHTHOUSE *SO THE LIGHT TOWER COULD DOUBLE AS A BELFRY*

THE **COFFINS** IN WHICH CHILDREN WERE BURIED BY THE ANCIENT GREEK INHABITANTS OF THE ISLAND OF ISCHIA *WERE USED WINE JUGS*

THESE HUNTERS REALLY USE THEIR HEADS

NUBA TRIBESMEN of the Sudan, Africa, AS RATIONS FOR LONG HUNTING TRIPS *WIND ROLLS OF MAIZE FLOUR AND BUTTER AROUND LOCKS OF THEIR HAIR*

THE NEST OF THE VIOLET-EARED HUMMINGBIRD OF South America IS ALWAYS CONSTRUCTED WITH *A CURTAIN* MADE OF BLADES OF GRASS. IT DEFLECTS RAIN

THE SEA LAMPREY BUILDS A NEST IN THE GRAVEL BED OF A STREAM BY SCOOPING OUT STONES AND CARRYING THEM AWAY IN HER MOUTH ONE BY ONE, THEN LAYS AS MANY AS *236,000 EGGS--AND IMMEDIATELY DIES*

THE COOKING VESSELS USED BY AMERICAN INDIANS WERE MADE OF BIRCH BARK OR THE SKINS OF ANIMALS AND THE WATER WAS BROUGHT TO A BOIL *BY TOSSING INTO IT RED HOT STONES*

CLARA FISHER (1811-1898) WHO FIRST APPEARED ON THE LONDON STAGE AT THE AGE OF 7 *WAS A POPULAR ACTRESS FOR 72 YEARS*

Dr. JAKOB RUHE (1767-1823) A SURGEON IN BERLIN, GERMANY, HAD 6 FINGERS ON EACH HAND AND 6 TOES ON EACH FOOT --AS DID EVERY MEMBER OF HIS FAMILY BEFORE HIM *FOR 6 GENERATIONS*

THE **MALE SEA SPIDER** HAS AN EXTRA PAIR OF LEGS WHICH ARE USED ONLY FOR CARRYING ITS MATE'S UNHATCHED EGGS

THE ALLIGATOR GAR *HAS SCALES AS SHINY AS ENAMEL AND AS HARD AS STEEL* THEY CAN RESIST THE BLOW OF A SHARP AXE

THE LONG TAIL OFTEN LINES ITS NEST WITH AS MANY AS **2,300 FEATHERS** *WHICH THE MOTHER PLUCKS FROM HER OWN COAT*

CHARLES COFFIN WHO BECAME PRESIDENT OF TUSCULUM COLLEGE, IN GREENEVILLE, TENN., READ THE BIBLE FROM COVER TO COVER TWICE *BEFORE HE WAS 10 YEARS OF AGE*

THE **CATHEDRAL** of ST. CIRIACUS IN ANCONA, ITALY, BUILT 1,400 YEARS AGO USED IN ITS CONSTRUCTION *THE WALLS OF A RUINED ROMAN TEMPLE*

HARETS ben **BILLIZET** 500-605, AN ARABIAN POET WHO LIVED TO THE AGE OF 105, NEVER VENTURED FROM HIS HOME UNLESS HIS FACE WAS COVERED *BY 7 VEILS*

A HILL THE **SINGING HILL of ONGON OBO**, Ordos Desert, China, THAT WHEN WALKED UPON *PRODUCES THE SOUND OF MUSIC*

THE STRANGEST DOG CALLS IN THE WORLD

SPEAKING DRUMS IN NEW GUINEA, HOLLOWED OUT TREE TRUNKS WHICH PRODUCE SOUNDS WHEN A STICK IS DRAGGED THROUGH A SLIT, ARE USED TO SUMMON THE OWNERS' DOGS *-EACH OF WHICH RECOGNIZES HIS OWN CALL*

THE EMPEROR WHO FORGOT THE NAME OF HIS OWN WIFE!

CHARLEMAGNE

IN DEDICATING A NEW IMPERIAL PALACE IN 800 HAD PLANNED TO NAME IT AFTER HIS WIFE, LINDGARD, TO WHOM HE HAD BEEN MARRIED FOR 6 YEARS *-BUT THROUGHOUT THE CEREMONIES HE COULD NOT REMEMBER HER NAME* HE FINALLY NAMED IT "UXOR" -- LATIN FOR "A WOMAN"

A **PAINT ROLLER** THAT WAS *"SWALLOWED UP" BY A TREE*

THE HUENIA

A CRAB FOUND IN THE GREAT BARRIER REEF OF AUSTRALIA LIVES ON THE HALIMEDA WEED BECAUSE IT IS *IDENTICAL IN SHAPE AND COLOR TO THE WEED'S FRONDS*

THE FISH THAT SIT UP

THE LEMON DAB, WHICH HUNTS FOR WORMS IN THE MUDDY BOTTOM OF THE WATER, LOCATES ITS PREY BY RAISING ITS HEAD *UNTIL IT LOOKS AS IF IT WERE SITTING UP*

THE GREAT TOWER
in Azpeitia, Spain,
IN WHICH ST. IGNATIUS OF
LOYOLA WAS BORN IN 1491,
HAS BEEN PRESERVED AS A
MEMORIAL TO THE FOUNDER
OF THE JESUIT ORDER
*BY BUILDING A
MONASTERY AROUND IT*

WOMEN of the Wa-teita
Tribe of E. Africa
WEAR MORE THAN
500 STRINGS OF BEADS
WEIGHING OVER 30 POUNDS
THEY WEAR THEM AROUND
THEIR WAIST, NECK AND ARMS

A SINGLE WING FEATHER
OF ANY BIRD
TO MAKE IT MORE EFFICIENT
IN FLIGHT HAS APPROXIMATELY
1,000,000 BARBS AND BARBULES

**PER.
HAKANSSON**
(1792-1829) of Sweden
KNEW THE 39 LANGUAGES OF EUROPE
*AS WELL AS
ARABIC and PERSIAN*

A **WILLOW TREE**
NEAR DORNBIRN, AUSTRIA,
*WITH A FIR TREE GROWING
OUT OF ITS CROWN*

HILAIRE GARDONA
(1878 - 1912)
A PARISIAN LAWYER
COULD ONLY READ WHEN
HE WAS HOLDING THE BOOK
UPSIDE DOWN

**GEORGE WASHINGTON
ROCK**, San Juan Islands,
near Seattle, Wash.
NATURAL STONE FORMATION

**ALEXANDER
MACARTHUR**
WAS ONE OF
7 BROTHERS
WHO FOUGHT
IN THE
BATTLE OF
CULLODEN,
SCOTLAND,
*AND THE ONLY
ONE OF THE 7
WHO SURVIVED*
April 16, 1746

HANGMAN'S ROCK ON COLONSAY ISLAND, IN THE HEBRIDES, SERVED FOR CENTURIES AS *A PUBLIC GALLOWS*

THE HOLE IN THE ROCK THROUGH WHICH THE ROPE WAS PASSED IS STILL VISIBLE

THOMAS **JORDAN** OF MANCHESTER, ENGLAND, NAMED HIS 5 SONS *"BE", "WITH", "YOU", "ALL" AND "AMEN"* --THE LAST 5 WORDS OF THE BIBLE

THE SWITCH TREE OF TAURANGA, N. Zealand, AN ASPEN WHICH GREW FROM A DROVER'S SWITCH *STUCK INTO THE GROUND 93 YEARS AGO*

FARMERS of Barétous, France, EACH JUNE 13th DELIVER 3 WHITE COWS TO THE FARMERS OF RONCAL, SPAIN --*A TRIBUTE THAT HAS BEEN CARRIED OUT FOR 596 YEARS*

THE BALANCING BOULDER OF CRAIGIE BARNS
A BOULDER in Dunkeld, Scotland,
13 FEET LONG, 7 FEET WIDE AND 5 FEET HIGH,
HAS BEEN BALANCING ON 3 TINY STONES
FOR 2,000,000 YEARS

THE
**OLDEST
ACER**

GEORGE
MILLER
of Anaheim,
Calif.,
MADE A
HOLE-IN-ONE
ON THE ANAHEIM
MUNICIPAL G.C.
AT THE AGE OF
93

AN **ICEBERG**
SIGHTED NEAR
MELVILLE BAY, IN THE
ARCTIC, IN 1883
*WAS SHAPED LIKE AN
ORIENTAL TEMPLE*

THE ARCH OF MARGARET WHICH STANDS IN FINALE, ITALY, WAS CONSTRUCTED IN 1947 FROM THE DEBRIS OF THE ORIGINAL ARCH ERECTED TO HONOR PRINCESS MARGARET OF SPAIN IN 1666 --AND DEMOLISHED IMMEDIATELY AFTER SHE HAD PASSED THROUGH IT

THE FRESHWATER WORM CAN BE CHOPPED INTO 40 PIECES --AND EACH PIECE WILL GROW A NEW HEAD AND TAIL

A **MOTHER** of Ruanda, Africa, WEARS A WHITE BAND ON HER HEAD --WHICH CANNOT BE REMOVED EXCEPT UPON THE DEATH OF HER HUSBAND OR THE KING

THE MT. ZION CHURCH CONSTRUCTED IN 1856 AND THE OLDEST PROTESTANT CHURCH IN ELK COUNTY, PA., HOLDS 2 SERVICES EACH YEAR...ON EASTER SUNDAY AND ON THE FIRST SUNDAY IN SEPTEMBER

JULIAN HAYDENEUFVE
(1588-1663)
THE FRENCH THEOLOGIAN
FOR 55 YEARS SLEPT ONLY
2 HOURS EACH NIGHT

RINGING THE BELLS
IN THE CHURCH ON MOUNT ISOLA,
ON AN ISLAND IN ISEO LAKE, ITALY,
IS BELIEVED TO ASSURE
GOOD FORTUNE AND HEALTH
--SO PILGRIMS CLIMB 2,000 FT.
AND PAY THE SEXTON A FEE
*FOR THE PRIVILEGE OF
PULLING THE BELL ROPE*

KAMCHATKA
BIGHORN SHEEP
HAVE TINY EARS, YET THEY
CAN INSTANTLY DETECT THE
DIRECTION OF ANY SOUND
BECAUSE THEIR HORNS
REINFORCE THEIR HEARING
IN THE MANNER OF A
*MAN CUPPING HIS
HAND TO HIS EAR*

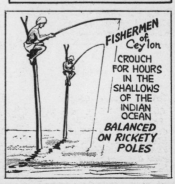

FISHERMEN of Ceylon CROUCH FOR HOURS IN THE SHALLOWS OF THE INDIAN OCEAN *BALANCED ON RICKETY POLES*

THE **7** CROSSES ATOP THE CHURCH OF BIR BIR MARYAM, IN CHINCHA, ETHIOPIA—EACH IS TOPPED BY *THE SHELL OF A REAL OSTRICH EGG*

"DANNY YOUNGER"

A PARAKEET OWNED BY MRS. ELLA HOHENSTEIN, OF ST. LOUIS, MISSOURI, WAS RETURNED AFTER BEING MISSING FOR 4 WEEKS BECAUSE HE KEPT REPEATING HIS NAME —*AND IT WAS LISTED IN THE TELEPHONE BOOK* THE LISTING ACTUALLY WAS THAT OF MRS. HOHENSTEIN'S GRANDSON, AFTER WHOM THE PARAKEET WAS NAMED

HARRY E. CRATE OF INGRAM, TEXAS, CAN DO **40** PUSHUPS AND STAND ON HIS HEAD *AT THE AGE OF* **81**

THE **MALE SEA HORSE** *CARRIES IN A POUCH,* UNTIL THEY HATCH, THE EGGS LAID BY ITS MATE— AS MANY AS 142 YOUNG SEA HORSES HAVE EMERGED IN A SINGLE YIELD

AN AMERICAN LANDING CRAFT DURING THE INVASION OF INCHON, IN NORTH KOREA, *WAS LEFT HIGH AND DRY BY A RECEDING 30-FOOT TIDE ATOP THE HULL OF AN OVERTURNED VESSEL*

KING JAJA'S PALACE IN OPOBO, NIGERIA, WAS CONSTRUCTED IN ENGLAND, THEN DISASSEMBLED AND SHIPPED TO ITS PRESENT SITE -*A DISTANCE OF 3,600 MILES*

MRS. JOHN FRANKLIN
SISTER-IN-LAW OF BENJAMIN FRANKLIN, WHO AS A WIDOW SUCCEEDED HER HUSBAND IN 1756 AS POSTMISTRESS OF BOSTON, WAS THE FIRST WOMAN IN NORTH AMERICA TO HOLD PUBLIC OFFICE

Dr. JAMES HAWES (1739-1821) of Westborough, Massachusetts, WAS A PHYSICIAN, LAWYER, FARMER, JUSTICE OF THE PEACE, TOWN CLERK, APOTHECARY, INNKEEPER, GROCER, DENTIST, CONSTABLE AND OPERATOR OF A LIVERY STABLE

THE ANT HOUSE PLANT
THE MYRMECODIA CONTAINS A MAZE OF GALLERIES INHABITED BY THOUSANDS OF ANTS -- WHICH REPAY THE PLANT'S HOSPITALITY BY *DEFENDING ITS LEAVES FROM PREDATORS*

THE GREAT GUN OF HUNZA
WAS MADE FOR THE RULER OF THE HIMALAYAN KINGDOM BY AN ITINERANT CHINESE GUNSMITH *OUT OF BRONZE AND COPPER POTS.* THE RULER PROMPTLY DECAPITATED THE GUNSMITH SO HE WOULD NOT BE ABLE TO MAKE A SIMILAR WEAPON FOR A RIVAL RULER

ABOUT **1,800 THUNDERSTORMS** A MINUTE OCCUR IN VARIOUS PARTS OF THE WORLD CONSTANTLY THROUGHOUT *EVERY DAY OF EVERY YEAR*

THE **CHURCH BELL** OF THE LOMA TRIBE OF WESTERN AFRICA CONSISTS OF A SPECIALLY FORGED *TIN PLATE*

EMPEROR KONG TI of China, FORCED TO DRINK A CUP OF POISON IN 619 AND PERMITTED TO UTTER A LAST PRAYER, FERVENTLY ASKED BUDDHA THAT IN HIS REINCARNATION *HE RETURN AS ANYTHING BUT AN EMPEROR*

FRANK FOSS of St. Petersburg, Fla. AT THE AGE OF 92 PLAYS BANJOS WHICH HE MAKES FROM *FRYING PANS*

129

PROFESSOR JAMES V.L. BLANEY
(1820 - 1874)
TAUGHT AT RUSH MEDICAL
COLLEGE, IN CHICAGO, AND AT
NORTHWESTERN UNIVERSITY,
IN EVANSTON, 20 MILES AWAY
--- *AT THE SAME TIME*

The **CASTLE OF DACHENSTEIN**
Austria
WAS BUILT IN THE 12 th CENTURY
SOLELY TO COVER A TREASURE
BURIED IN AN EXCAVATION IN
THE SOLID ROCK BENEATH IT
--*BUT NO ONE HAS EVER
FOUND THE TREASURE*

The **CHURCH** of **ST. PETER** in Portovenere, Italy,
WAS BUILT ATOP AN ANCIENT HEATHEN TEMPLE
--*THE RUINS OF WHICH ARE STILL INSIDE THE CHURCH*

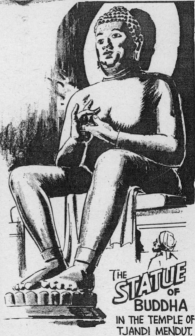

THE **GREAT** BERING GLACIER
AS IT MOVES THROUGH
A GAP IN THE
ST. ELIAS MOUNTAIN
RANGE, ALASKA,
TAKES THE SHAPE OF
A SPINNING TOP

THE **5 CHAPELS**
of the Capucine Church,
in Rome, Italy
ARE LINED WITH HUMAN
SKELETONS AND BONES
-*SOME OF THE SKELETONS*
ATTIRED AS MONKS

THE **STATUE** OF **BUDDHA**
IN THE TEMPLE OF
TJANDI MENDUT,
INDONESIA,
IS WORSHIPED BY LEAPS AND BOUNDS—
IT IS BELIEVED THAT ANYONE WHO CAN
JUMP HIGH ENOUGH TO TOUCH THE
BUDDHA'S HANDS--10 FEET ABOVE THE
GROUND--WILL BE GRANTED 7 WISHES

THE **FLOATING** ISLANDS OF BAVARIA
LAKE ARBER
HAS 3 LARGE ISLANDS
*WHICH MOVE TO AND FRO
WITH THE WIND*

THE KLIP SPRINGER
African Antelope
HAS SUCH SMALL FEET THAT
*ITS 4 HOOVES CAN FIT
ON A DIME*

ALBERT
BONJEAN
(1858 - 1939)
THE
BELGIAN
POET WAS
HONORED
BY THE
DEDICATION
OF A
MONUMENT
IN HIS
HONOR AT
VERVIERS,
BELGIUM,
*DURING
HIS
LIFETIME*

LION ROCK
ISLAND OF LIPARI, ITALY,
*NATURAL STONE
FORMATION*

KING ANAYATULLAH KHAN
of Afghanistan
WAS FORCED TO ABDICATE IN
1929 AFTER HE HAD BEEN ON
THE THRONE **ONLY 3 DAYS**

THE **MALE NEW GUINEA KURTUS**
CARRIES ITS MATE'S EGGS
UNTIL THEY HATCH, TIED BY
**COILED THREADS TO A BONY
HOOK ON ITS FOREHEAD**

THE **HERMITAGE of ST. ADRIAN**
WHICH HE CONSTRUCTED IN THE
TUNNEL OF ST. ADRIAN, SPAIN,
1,400 YEARS AGO, NOW SERVES
AS A POLICE STATION

A **PERSIMMON
STICK**
WHICH BY
GROWING THROUGH
A RATTAN VINE
ACQUIRED THE
SHAPE OF
A CORKSCREW
Owned by
Bob Zirkle
Parkin, Ark.

MR. **BLOOD** IS
CORONER
of Will County, Ill.

133

THE RIDING SCHOOL OF SALZBURG
Austria
ORIGINALLY CONSTRUCTED AS A BULLRING CONTAINS 3 HUGE ROWS OF 96 ARCADES EACH AND *WAS CARVED OUT OF THE SOLID ROCK OF A MOUNTAIN*

THE BEE HAS 3 INDEPENDENT BRAINS AND CAN FLY AND WALK AFTER ITS HEAD HAS BEEN SEVERED

THE MASTER MOOCHER
CARL ISRAEL HALLMAN (1732-1800)
ONE OF SWEDEN'S MOST SUCCESSFUL PLAYWRIGHTS, BOASTED THAT DURING HIS ENTIRE LIFETIME *HE NEVER PAID THE CHECK FOR A MEAL*

THE RUFF HAS SUCH A VARIANCE IN ITS PLUMAGE *THAT NO TWO ARE EXACTLY ALIKE*

THE FIRST WARNING OF OUR URBAN PROBLEMS
SOLON (638-555 B.C.) THE ATHENIAN LAWMAKER DECREED THAT NO TOWN COULD EXCEED A POPULATION OF 20,000 *TO AVOID "URBAN SPRAWL AND DECAY"* GREECE ENFORCED THIS LAW FOR MANY CENTURIES

ANTHONY HAMPTON of So. Carolina, *HAD 5 SONS WHO BECAME OFFICERS IN THE AMERICAN REVOLUTION* THEY WERE THE ONLY SURVIVORS IN THE FAMILY OF A BRITISH-INSPIRED INDIAN MASSACRE THAT KILLED THEIR FATHER, BROTHER, MOTHER AND A NEPHEW

THE DOORKNOCKERS OF PALATIAL HOMES IN MOROCCO ARE METAL MOULDINGS OF *THE HANDS OF THE YOUNGEST WOMAN IN THE HOUSE*

JOHN NEVISON, A HIGHWAYMAN, AFTER ROBBING A STAGE ON A HIGHWAY NEAR LONDON, ENGLAND, RODE ALL THE WAY TO YORK TO SET UP AN ALIBI *COVERING 190 MILES IN 15 HOURS* (1676)

THE CONCORDIA TEMPLE in Agrigento, Italy, WAS BUILT 2,400 YEARS AGO AS A GREEK TEMPLE, SERVED AS A CHRISTIAN CHURCH FOR 1,200 YEARS -- *THEN WAS CONVERTED INTO A GREEK TEMPLE*

KING MUSHIDI

RULER OF GARENGANZE, AFRICA, FROM 1856 TO 1891, ALWAYS SIGNED ROYAL DOCUMENTS WITH HIS FULL NAME *MUSHIDI, SAIDI, MARIA SECUNDA, VICTORIA*

THE 60 COLUMNS LINING THE COURTYARD OF THE PRINCE BISHOPS' PALACE, IN LIEGE, BELGIUM— *EACH WAS CARVED IN A DIFFERENT DESIGN BY ONE OF 60 SCULPTORS*

A *SALT BASKET* USED 2,400 YEARS AGO IN Hallstatt, Austria, WAS FOUND TO HAVE ATTACHED TO IT A "REST POLE" WHICH ENABLED ITS CARRIER TO SUPPORT HIS BASKET DURING REST PERIODS WITHOUT TAKING IT OFF HIS SHOULDERS

HOMES on the island of Lewis, in the Hebrides, BECAUSE THERE WAS NO LIME IN THE AREA WERE BUILT OF STONES WITHOUT MORTAR *- MANY OF THE WALLS BEING 6 FEET THICK*

AN AGED PERSON THAT HAD SEEN BUT NINETEEN WINTERS IN THE WORLD

EPITAPH of NATHANAEL MATHER *WHO GRADUATED FROM HARVARD AT 16 AND DIED 3 YEARS LATER* Charter St. Cemetery, Salem, Mass.

THE CHURCH OF GOTHENBURG in Sweden CONSTRUCTED IN 1748 IS USED FOR WEDDINGS AND FUNERALS *BUT HOLDS NO REGULAR SERVICES*

LOVE SPOONS ELABORATELY CARVED, ONCE WERE GIVEN BY WELSH SWAINS TO THEIR SWEETHEARTS *IN LIEU OF ENGAGEMENT RINGS*

137

A HOME
IN ARZACHENA, SARDINIA, THAT WAS *HOLLOWED OUT OF A GIANT BOULDER—* A DOOR WAS BUILT INTO THE BOULDER AND ITS OUTER WALL IS COVERED WITH SMALL STONES AS A DECORATIVE GESTURE

CHRISTOPHER MOEDERL
of Rosenheim, Germany, CLIMBING A FENCE ON HIS WAY TO TAKE HIS RIFLE TO A GUNSMITH FOR REPAIR, SLIPPED, ACCIDENTALLY DISCHARGED THE WEAPON, *AND WITH A SINGLE SHOT KILLED 2 FOXES*

THE ALARM
SOUNDED BY SIDAMO WATCHMEN IN THE FIELDS OF ETHIOPIA *IS ON A HANDMADE XYLOPHONE -- WHICH CAN BE HEARD A MILE DISTANT*

WINDOW PLANT
(Haworthia *retusa*)
A SOUTH AFRICAN PLANT HAS TRANSPARENT LEAVES *WHICH ADMIT SUNLIGHT TO THE PLANT'S INTERIOR*

ALEXANDER HARDY (1560-1631)
FRENCH DRAMATIC AUTHOR WROTE 600 THREE-ACT PLAYS *--EACH OF WHICH HE COMPLETED IN A SINGLE WEEK*

THE HEART of KING ROBERT BRUCE OF SCOTLAND LOST ON A MOORISH BATTLE-FIELD WHILE BEING TRANSPORTED ON A PILGRIMAGE TO THE HOLY LAND, WAS *RECOVERED YEARS LATER AND BURIED IN THE CHANCEL OF MELROSE ABBEY, SCOTLAND*

HEART of BRUCE

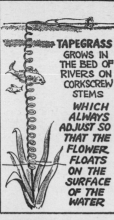

TAPEGRASS GROWS IN THE BED OF RIVERS ON CORKSCREW STEMS *WHICH ALWAYS ADJUST SO THAT THE FLOWER FLOATS ON THE SURFACE OF THE WATER*

CARL A. WALDMAN OF READING, PA., WAS HIT BY A TRUCK AT THE CORNER OF 11th AND SPRING STREETS, READING --*AT THE SAME TIME AS HIS SON, MICHAEL, 11, WAS INJURED BY A CAR AT THE CORNER OF 10th AND SPRING STREETS*- THEY WERE TAKEN TO THE SAME HOSPITAL AT THE SAME MOMENT -- BUT NEITHER WAS SERIOUSLY HURT

Amos A. LAWRENCE (1814-1886) A N.Y. PHILANTHROPIST *HAS A KANSAS TOWN AND 2 UNIVERSITIES NAMED AFTER HIM--* THE TOWN IS LAWRENCE, KANS., AND THE SCHOOLS ARE LAWRENCE UNIV., IN KANSAS, AND LAWRENCE UNIV. IN APPLETON, WISC. --A TOWN NAMED FOR HIS WIFE'S FAMILY

THE PASS GIVEN TO SOLDIERS OF MEMMINGEN, GERMANY, IN THE 15th CENTURY CONSISTED OF THE LETTER "M"--*PAINTED WITH RED INK ON A THUMBNAIL*

THE **EGG** OF A MOA, EXTINCT BIRD OF New Zealand, RESTORED FROM 200 FRAGMENTS FOUND IN 1939 *IS 7 INCHES LONG AND 5 INCHES WIDE*

OH HE WAS A GOOD IF E'ER A GOOD BOY LIVED

EPITAPH ON Block Island, Rhode Island, FOR A CHILD WHO DIED IN 1885, AT 10 --*BUT WHOSE NAME WAS LEFT OFF HIS GRAVESTONE*

A **WAR** GALLEY
170 FEET LONG, ARMED WITH
104 CANNON AND MANNED
BY 104 ROWERS, WAS
CONSTRUCTED TO HONOR
KING LOUIS XIV'S VISIT TO
A TOULON SHIPYARD
*DURING THE DAYLIGHT HOURS
OF A SINGLE DAY*   (1679)

THE **"OLDEST AMERICAN!"**
SYLVESTER MAGEE,
of Columbia, Miss.,
FOUGHT ON BOTH SIDES IN
THE CIVIL WAR, BECAME A
FATHER AT THE AGE OF 109
AND AT THE TIME THIS IS WRITTEN
IS IN EXCELLENT HEALTH
AT THE AGE OF 129 !
HIS BIRTH ON MAY 29, 1841, HAS
BEEN OFFICIALLY ATTESTED BY
THE STATE OF MISSISSIPPI

THE **SALEM REFORMED CHURCH**
In Cincinnati, Ohio,
WAS CONSTRUCTED AS AN EXACT
DUPLICATE OF A CHURCH IN
FRANKFURT-ON-THE-MAIN, GERMANY

THE **STRANGEST GUNNER IN ALL HISTORY** "Kubadar Moll," AN ELEPHANT USED TO TRANSPORT CANNON IN THE BATTLE OF LUCKNOW, INDIA, WHEN AN ENTIRE GUN CREW BECAME DISABLED, TOOK THE TORCH FROM A WOUNDED GRENADIER AND *FIRED ONE OF THE CANNON-* THE ELEPHANT'S ACTION HELD UP THE ENEMY LONG ENOUGH FOR THE ARRIVAL OF REINFORCEMENTS (1858)

JAMES WHITTAKER GEYER of Bucyrus, Ohio, WALKED UNAIDED AT THE AGE OF 6½ MONTHS

STEAMSHIPS BUILT IN A SHIPYARD IN GREIFSWALD, GERMANY, FOR 100 YEARS HAD TO BE TRANSPORTED THROUGH THE CITY ON GREAT TRAILERS PULLED BY HORSES *--BECAUSE THE SHIPYARD WAS LOCATED FAR FROM THE WATER*

JEAN HARDOUIN (1646-1729)
A MEMBER OF THE JESUIT ORDER
FOR 67 YEARS, HAD A LIBRARY OF
12,000 BOOKS ON SUCH SUBJECTS
AS ANTIQUITY AND PHILOSOPHY
-- *THE ENTIRE CONTENTS OF
WHICH HE MEMORIZED FROM
COVER TO COVER*

THE **CASTLE** of **HAVRÉ**
NEAR MONS, BELGIUM,
CONSTRUCTED IN MEDIEVAL TIMES,
HAS BEEN SINKING INTO THE
WATER AT THE RATE OF
6 INCHES EACH YEAR

JOHN McCLUNG
of Hesperia, Calif.,
PLAYING GOLF AT THE HESPERIA C.C.
*ACED THE 150-YARD 14th HOLE
3 TIMES IN 11 MONTHS*

A **GREAT NORTHERN PIKE**
WEIGHING 16 POUNDS
CAUGHT BY GEORGE POWER,
IN GREEN LAKE, MINN.
*HAD SWALLOWED CROSS
LINKS FROM 3 DIFFERENT
SIZE SETS OF TIRE CHAINS
AND A 1½-INCH EYEBOLT*

A MONUMENT TO OPTIMISM

THE MEMORIAL CONSTRUCTED BY CHIEF VAOVASA, of Manono, in Samoa, TO HIS WIVES CONTAINS 99 STONES, ONE FOR EACH OF HIS WIVES, AND HAS A SPACE FOR THE 100th STONE— *BUT VAOVASA WAS SLAIN BEFORE HE COULD COMPLETE HIS GOAL*

THE **GUILLOTINE** in Paris, France, ON WHICH SO MANY NOBLEMEN DIED DURING THE FRENCH REVOLUTION *WAS SOLD AT AUCTION IN 1914*

THE **STONE LIGHTHOUSE** near Prescott, Canada, *WAS ORIGINALLY CONSTRUCTED AS A WINDMILL*

"PEACE AND PLENTY"
WAS THE NAME OF THIS STRUCTURE IN HUNTINGTON, N.Y. WHICH FOR YEARS CATERED TO STAGECOACH PASSENGERS

The **TOMBSTONE** in Otley, England, OVER THE GRAVE OF WORKERS KILLED IN THE CONSTRUCTION OF THE BRAMHOPE TUNNEL *IS SHAPED LIKE THE ENTRANCE TO THAT TUNNEL*

THE TOWN GATE of Cuzco, Peru, WAS BUILT WITH HEWN STONE *OBTAINED BY DEMOLISHING ANCIENT INCA STRUCTURES*

The **NEST** OF THE REED BUNTING CONSISTS OF BLADES OF GRASS WOVEN AROUND A TRIPOD OF 3 STURDY REEDS –AND THE STRONGEST WINDS *CANNOT DEMOLISH IT*

FALSE **SCORPIONS** SMALL ANIMALS RESEMBLING SCORPIONS ATTACH THEMSELVES TO THE LEGS OF FLIES *SOLELY AS A MEANS OF TRANSPORTATION*

144

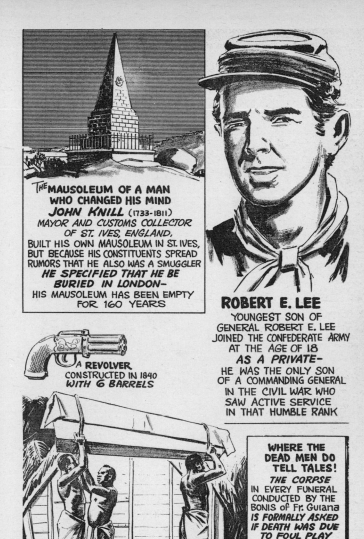

THE **MAUSOLEUM OF A MAN WHO CHANGED HIS MIND** *JOHN KNILL* (1733-1811) MAYOR AND CUSTOMS COLLECTOR OF ST. IVES, ENGLAND, BUILT HIS OWN MAUSOLEUM IN ST. IVES, BUT BECAUSE HIS CONSTITUENTS SPREAD RUMORS THAT HE ALSO WAS A SMUGGLER *HE SPECIFIED THAT HE BE BURIED IN LONDON—* HIS MAUSOLEUM HAS BEEN EMPTY FOR 160 YEARS

A REVOLVER CONSTRUCTED IN 1840 *WITH 6 BARRELS*

ROBERT E. LEE

YOUNGEST SON OF GENERAL ROBERT E. LEE JOINED THE CONFEDERATE ARMY AT THE AGE OF 18 *AS A PRIVATE—* HE WAS THE ONLY SON OF A COMMANDING GENERAL IN THE CIVIL WAR WHO SAW ACTIVE SERVICE IN THAT HUMBLE RANK

WHERE THE DEAD MEN DO TELL TALES! *THE CORPSE* IN EVERY FUNERAL CONDUCTED BY THE BONIS of Fr. Guiana *IS FORMALLY ASKED IF DEATH WAS DUE TO FOUL PLAY*

THE MEN CARRYING THE COFFIN INSIST THAT IF THE ANSWER IS "YES," THEY WILL FEEL THE CORPSE TILT FORWARD

MANY PUBLIC FOUNTAINS IN Barcelona, Spain, DOUBLE AS *LIGHT POLES*

THE *ACCURSE* CHAPEL in Arles, France, WAS CONSTRUCTED IN 1520 BY ANTOINE de BEAUJEU AS ATONEMENT FOR HAVING *KILLED AN OPPONENT IN A DUEL*— HE ALSO MADE PROVISION FOR DAILY PRAYERS FOR HIS VICTIM *FOR THE NEXT 273 YEARS*

SAMUEL WOODWORTH COZZENS (1834-1878) PLUNGED **300** FEET IN THE VALLEY of ZUÑI, N.M., FROM A STEEP, ROCKY PRECIPICE AND *SUFFERED NO INJURIES EXCEPT A BROKEN ARM*

HARVEY NICKERSON
ONE OF THE ONLY TWO SURVIVORS WHEN THE CANADIAN SHIP "PORT CLYDE" WAS SWEPT BY YELLOW FEVER IN 1875 WAS ONLY 23 YEARS OLD -BUT *HIS BLACK HAIR TURNED WHITE IN A SINGLE NIGHT*

AN **1,100-YEAR-OLD MYSTERY**
A GRAVE UNCOVERED IN HENCIDA, HUNGARY, WAS FOUND TO CONTAIN *A PAGAN WOMAN AND HER HORSE*
THE PAGANS ALWAYS BURIED A GREAT WARRIOR WITH HIS HORSE --BUT THIS IS THE ONLY KNOWN INSTANCE OF A WOMAN BEING GIVEN THIS HONOR

THE FATHER OF ACADEMIC FASHION
ROBERT of KETENE
A 12th-CENTURY ENGLISH SCHOLAR WHO STUDIED AT THE UNIVERSITY of PAMPLONA, SPAIN, BROUGHT BACK TO ENGLAND A LONG ARAB GOWN --*WHICH BECAME THE ACADEMIC ROBE OF ALL WESTERN UNIVERSITIES*

THE **TARAHUMARE INDIANS**
of Mexico
FISH IN THE FUERTE RIVER
WITH BLANKETS

WOMEN in China

WORKING AS STREET SWEEPERS *OFTEN CARRY THEIR BABIES IN A SLING ON THEIR BACK*

THE **HOME** of AUGUSTO MATTOS
near Coimbra, Portugal,
WAS CONSTRUCTED ON TOP OF AN ANCIENT STONE FURNACE
MATTOS SELECTED THE SITE TO PRESERVE THE FURNACE, IN WHICH LEGEND SAYS A KING ONCE BURNED TO DEATH A DISLOYAL AIDE

Cat
BORN WITH 3 LEGS

THE LARVA OF A CADDIS FLY CATCHES FOOD FROM THE WATER BY *WEAVING A LARGE NET*

THE ROUND HOUSE in Fremantle, Australia ALSO KNOWN AS THE OCTAGON HOUSE *ACTUALLY IS NEITHER ROUND NOR OCTAGONAL* IT HAS 12 SIDES

"DADDY LONGLEGS" HAS **8** LEGS *EACH 10 TIMES AS LONG AS ITS BODY*

GLACIER EGGS HUGE ROCKS GROUND BY GLACIERS FOR THOUSANDS OF YEARS INTO THE SHAPE OF *MONSTROUS EGGS*

DR. FELIX MARQUIER of St. Lo, France, BECAUSE HE SAVED VICTIMS OF A PLAGUE THAT HAD LASTED FOR 30 YEARS *WAS CONVICTED OF SORCERY AND SENTENCED TO DEATH—* THE FRENCH PARLIAMENT FINALLY REDUCED THE SENTENCE IN 1661 TO ETERNAL BANISHMENT FROM HIS NATIVE LAND

AFRICAN ITYRAEA BUTTERFLIES SETTLE ON A STEM IN LARGE GROUPS -- *CREATING THE APPEARANCE OF A FLOWERING PLANT*

THE HUMAN EAGLE

THE MARQUIS de BACQUEVILLE in Paris, France, IN 1742 USING THE WINGS OF AN EAGLE LEAPED FROM THE ROOF OF HIS HOUSE AND *ACTUALLY FLEW A DISTANCE OF 700 FEET* HE LANDED ON A RIVER BOAT AND SUFFERED A BROKEN LEG

THE GATEWAY To Mombasa, Kenya, THROUGH WHICH ALL TRAFFIC MUST PASS, IS FORMED BY *2 PAIRS OF GIGANTIC ELEPHANT TUSKS*

THE SMALLEST STEER IN THE WORLD A STEER BORN IN ALTOONA, PA., IN 1914 GREW TO A HEIGHT OF ONLY *26 INCHES*

THE HAVEN TAVERN in Shrewsbury, Mass., WAS DISMANTLED IN 1871 TO PROVIDE A SITE FOR THE TOWN HALL, AND *SECTIONS OF THE OLD INN BECAME 3 HOMES LOCATED IN VARIOUS PARTS OF THE COMMUNITY*

NOCTILUCA MILIARIS SO TINY THAT HUNDREDS ARE IN A DROP OF WATER, *IS RESPONSIBLE FOR THE PHOSPHORESCENCE OF THE SEA*

JEAN-JACQUES de CAMBACÉRÈS (1753-1824) THE FRENCH STATESMAN, BECAUSE THE NUMERALS IN THE YEAR OF HIS BIRTH ADD UP TO 16 *ATE 16 ENTREES AND 16 DESSERTS AT DINNER EVERY DAY OF HIS ADULT LIFE*

KARL WITTE (1800-1883) WAS A PHILOSOPHY MAJOR IN THE UNIVERSITY OF GIESSEN, GERMANY, AT THE AGE OF 9 ½ *AND RECEIVED HIS Ph.D. AT 14*

Lady willing to give corporal punishment to widower's 3 girls. Good salary. State age and experience.

CLASSIFIED AD IN A NEWSPAPER IN CHRISTCHURCH, N.Z., ON JAN. 15, 1903

THE SHIP THAT COULD ONLY POSTPONE ITS DOOM!

The "C.S. HOLMES" BEING SWEPT TOWARD THE ROCKY COAST OF VANCOUVER ISLAND DURING A GALE IN 1909, WAS MIRACULOUSLY SAVED BY A CHANGE IN THE DIRECTION OF THE WIND *41 YEARS LATER ANOTHER GALE WRECKED THE SHIP EXACTLY IN THE SAME POSITION*

THE MULTILINGUAL LIPREADER

MRS. MARTHA REINERS (1860-1904) of Vienna, Austria, WHO WAS DEAF FROM BIRTH, COULD READ LIPS AND UNDERSTAND *GERMAN, CZECH, FRENCH AND ENGLISH*

JOHANN FROBEN (1460-1527)

A PRINTER AND PUBLISHER IN BASEL, SWITZERLAND, *WAS THE FIRST PUBLISHER TO PAY AN AUTHOR IN CASH-* UNTIL FROBEN GAVE ERASMUS A SUM IN CASH FOR HIS BOOK, "ADAGIA," IN 1513, ALL AUTHORS WERE GIVEN COPIES OF THEIR OWN BOOK -- *WHICH THEY WERE PERMITTED TO SELL AS THEIR PAYMENT*

LOUISA ADLER
DIED 1933
AGE 60
DIED OF GRIEF
CAUSED BY
A NEIGHBOR
NOW RESTS
IN PEACE

Epitaph in Palm Springs, Calif.

THE MAN WHO IS PROUD TO BE CALLED A MURDERER

Ibrahim ben Chem of El Golea, Algeria, A BANDIT WHO WAS PARDONED BY THE FRENCH GOVERNMENT IS DELIGHTED WITH THE NICKNAME HE ALWAYS USES: *"THE MAN OF 45 MURDERS"*

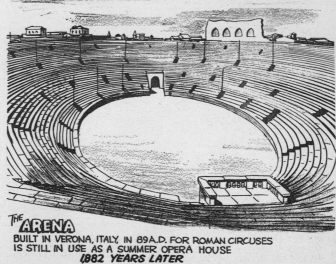

THE ARENA
BUILT IN VERONA, ITALY, IN 89 A.D. FOR ROMAN CIRCUSES IS STILL IN USE AS A SUMMER OPERA HOUSE *1,882 YEARS LATER*

POLICE CLUBS
CARRIED DURING THE
FRENCH REVOLUTION
WERE MADE OF SOLID IVORY

LOI·DU·29·7bre·1791

OFFICIER·DE·PAIX·

THE
ESCHENHEIMER TOWER

IN FRANKFURT ON THE MAIN, GERMANY,
WAS LONG THE SUBJECT OF A PUZZLE
WHICH EXPOSED IMPOSTORS CLAIMING TO BE FROM THAT CITY—
ASKED "WHAT HAS 5 POINTS, YET WILL NEVER HURT YOU?"
A NATIVE ALWAYS ANSWERS "**THE ESCHENHEIMER TOWER**"

A
CITY
COMPRISING
200 HOMES
AND A CHURCH
WAS BUILT INSIDE THE WALLS OF THE OLD ROMAN CIRCUS AT ARLES, FRANCE
THE CITY, CREATED FROM THE STONES USED AS SEATS IN THE
ANCIENT AMPHITHEATRE, ENDURED FOR 1,000 YEARS

154

THE **MOST REMARKABLE RIVER IN THE WORLD**
THE **LLYFNI RIVER**
of Wales
FLOWS THROUGH THE CENTER
OF LAKE LLANGORSE,
YET THEIR WATERS NEVER MIX
*– AND THE FISH OF ONE
ARE NEVER FOUND
IN THE OTHER*

THE **COVERED WOODEN BRIDGE** of **PANZENDORF** in Tyrol
BUILT BY A GROUP OF GERMAN EMIGRANTS
PASSING THROUGH THE AREA EN ROUTE TO ITALY
-- IS STILL IN USE 800 YEARS LATER

HANS CHRISTIAN ANDERSEN
THE FAMED DANISH CREATOR
OF FAIRY STORIES
WHEN HE DIED IN 1875
AT THE AGE OF **70**
WAS FOUND TO BE
CARRYING IN A LEATHER
CASE OVER HIS HEART
A LOVE LETTER WRITTEN
TO HIM 45 YEARS BEFORE BY
RIBORG VOIGT--*WHO JILTED
HIM TO MARRY ANOTHER*

The "AURORA" and "MAKAWELI"

2 BARKENTINES WHICH LEFT SYDNEY, AUSTRALIA, ON OCT. 8, 1915, REACHED CAPE FLATTERY, WASH., AFTER TRAVELING 9,000 MI. AND FOR 67 DAYS, *AT THE SAME TIME!*

THE CLOWNFISH
A NATURAL PREY BECAUSE OF ITS BRILLIANT COLORS HIDES FROM PREDATORS BY DARTING INSIDE THE EQUALLY BRIGHT HUED TENTACLES *OF A SEA ANEMONE*

THE NEST of
a South American CATERPILLAR IS A SILKEN COCOON SUSPENDED FROM A LEAF ON A LONG SILKEN CORD AND *IT SERVES AS A CRADLE AND AS A REPOSITORY FOR THE CATERPILLAR'S SKIN DURING ITS METAMORPHOSIS TO A BUTTERFLY*

NICHOLAS FRERET
(1688-1749) of Paris, France, CREATED **30** DICTIONARIES *--EACH IN A DIFFERENT LANGUAGE*

156

THE SILVER DART

WAS THE FIRST PLANE EVER FLOWN IN THE BRITISH EMPIRE— IT REACHED AN ALTITUDE OF 60 FEET AND STAYED ALOFT FOR THREE QUARTERS OF A MILE AT BADDECK, NOVA SCOTIA, ON FEB. 23, 1909

THE PAGODA of the ROYAL PET

THE MAHARANI of Jeypour, India, AS A TOMB FOR HER DOG *ERECTED A MAGNIFICENT MARBLE MEMORIAL WITH 4 COLUMNS AND A CUPOLA*

THE HONEST LIAR

GEN. ADOLPHUS WASHINGTON GREELY (1844-1935) REJECTED 3 TIMES BY THE UNION ARMY BECAUSE HE REFUSED TO LIE ABOUT HIS AGE, FINALLY WAS ACCEPTED WHEN HE CHALKED AN "18" ON THE SOLE OF EACH SHOE AND WHEN ASKED HIS AGE SAID: **" I'M OVER 18 "** HE BECAME THE FIRST AMERICAN SOLDIER TO RISE FROM PRIVATE TO GENERAL

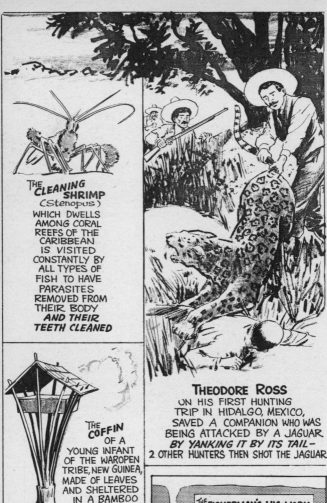

THE CLEANING SHRIMP
(Stenopus)

WHICH DWELLS AMONG CORAL REEFS OF THE CARIBBEAN IS VISITED CONSTANTLY BY ALL TYPES OF FISH TO HAVE PARASITES REMOVED FROM THEIR BODY *AND THEIR TEETH CLEANED*

THE COFFIN
OF A YOUNG INFANT OF THE WAROPEN TRIBE, NEW GUINEA, MADE OF LEAVES AND SHELTERED IN A BAMBOO STAND, *IS EXHIBITED NEAR THE HOME OF THE DEAD CHILD'S PARENTS FOR A PERIOD OF 10 YEARS*

THEODORE ROSS
ON HIS FIRST HUNTING TRIP IN HIDALGO, MEXICO, SAVED A COMPANION WHO WAS BEING ATTACKED BY A JAGUAR *BY YANKING IT BY ITS TAIL—* 2 OTHER HUNTERS THEN SHOT THE JAGUAR

THE FISHERMAN'S LUG WORM
DIGS AN "L" SHAPED BURROW WHICH IT CONSTANTLY ENLARGES *BY EATING SAND-- TO CONSUME SMALL WORMS IN THE GROUND*

MADDALENA GRANNATA of Naples, Italy, HAD NO OFFSPRING IN HER FIRST MARRIAGE BUT BORE HER SECOND HUSBAND **62 CHILDREN**

SHE HAD 11 SETS OF TRIPLETS, 4 SETS OF QUADRUPLETS, ONE SET OF QUINTUPLETS--AND HAD HER 62d CHILD AT THE AGE OF 57

EDGAR DEGAS (1834-1917) THE CELEBRATED FRENCH PAINTER *WAS TERRIFIED OF FLOWERS AND PERFUME-* THE SIGHT AND SCENT OF EITHER MADE HIM GRAVELY ILL

THE **MILLIPEDE** IS A VEGETARIAN BUT

THE **CENTIPEDE** IS A FEROCIOUS *MEAT EATER*

TEAPOT DOME ROCK *NATURAL STONE FORMATION in Wyoming*

THE CHURCH of LOEX in France
HAS NEVER BEEN USED FOR ANY SERVICE
EXCEPT FUNERALS

THE **MALAYAN MANTIS**
NORMALLY IS PINK,
PURPLE AND WHITE,
WITH GREEN STRIPES
--BUT WHEN DANGER
THREATENS IT CAN
CHANGE TO THE COLORS
*OF ANY ORCHID ON
WHICH IT HAS SETTLED*

JAMES WATTIE (1789-1872)
PARISH SCHOOLMASTER
of Crimond, Scotland,
ALWAYS WORE 3 SETS OF FLANNEL
UNDERWEAR AND 4 GREATCOATS
ONE ON TOP OF THE OTHER
*- EVEN DURING THE HOTTEST
DAYS OF SUMMER*

PIERRE de VILLARS
(1545-1613)
WAS THE HEAD OF
THE MONASTERY OF MIRIBEL, FRANCE,
AT THE AGE OF 8

THE **TROPICAL CELYPHID FLY**
TO FRIGHTEN
AWAY PREDATORS
PUFFS ITSELF UP
TO LOOK LIKE
A BEETLE

THE FIRST DRONE PLANE

A PIGGYBACK PLANE INVENTED BY THE GERMANS IN 1943, WAS LOADED WITH HIGH EXPLOSIVES AND CARRIED ON TOP OF ANOTHER PLANE -- *THEN STEERED BY REMOTE CONTROL TO ITS TARGET*

PISTOLS MADE IN ITALY IN THE 17th CENTURY *DOUBLED AS A KNIFE AND FORK*

THE SURGEON WHOSE FEE SET THE PRECEDENT

DR. CHARLES-FRANÇOIS FELIX

(1642-1703) CHIEF SURGEON TO KING LOUIS XIV of France FOR PERFORMING A FISTULA OPERATION ON THE RULER IN 1687 *RECEIVED THE EQUIVALENT TODAY OF $7,000,000, A MAGNIFICENT ESTATE AND A TITLE OF NOBILITY*

POHUTUKAWA TREES

WHICH GROW IN A CREEK BOTTOM NEAR GOAT ISLAND, N.Z., ASSUME THE MOST GROTESQUE SHAPES IN NATURE -- YET THEY ARE USED AS *CHRISTMAS TREES IN N. ZEALAND*

THE ARCH OF GAVI
in Verona, Italy,
DESTROYED BY NAPOLEON TO
FACILITATE HIS ARMY'S ENTRANCE
INTO VERONA IN 1797,
WAS REBUILT 138 YEARS LATER
WITH THE ORIGINAL STONES

STEFANO KUBRE
A SCHOLAR
OF MILAN, ITALY,
COULD NOT READ A BOOK
UNLESS HE LOOKED AT IT
*OVER THE SHOULDER OF
THE MAN HOLDING IT*

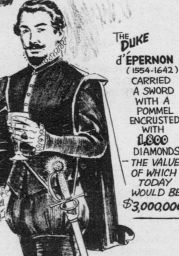

THE **DUKE
d'ÉPERNON**
(1554-1642)
CARRIED
A SWORD
WITH A
POMMEL
ENCRUSTED
WITH
1,800
DIAMONDS
— *THE VALUE
OF WHICH
TODAY
WOULD BE*
$3,000,000

MALLARDS
LEAVING THEIR NEST IN
SEARCH OF FOOD, PROTECT
THEIR EGGS AGAINST COLD
AND PREDATORS BY A
BLANKET OF FEATHERS PULLED
FROM THE MOTHER'S OWN BODY

THE **WHEELOCK HOUSE** – FIRST HOME IN WHAT IS NOW SHREWSBURY, MASS., WAS CONSTRUCTED BY GERSHOM WHEELOCK *WHO BUILT IT WITHOUT HELP IN A SINGLE WINTER*

TRANSPLANTED

Epitaph of LORENZO SABINE IN HILLSIDE CEMETERY, EASTPORT, ME.

THE **MAN** WHOSE HEART PERFORMED AN ACT OF COMPASSION EVEN IN DEATH

GEORGE (1669-1705) RULER OF HESSEN, GERMANY, WAS KILLED IN THE BATTLE OF BARCELONA AFTER HAVING CONQUERED GIBRALTAR FOR THE BRITISH, BUT HIS EMBALMED HEART WAS SEIZED BY A FRENCH WARSHIP AND HELD FOR RANSOM BY KING LOUIS XIV OF FRANCE—

SIX YEARS LATER IT WAS FINALLY EXCHANGED FOR 20 IMPRISONED FRENCH NAVAL OFFICERS

MOUNT TARAWERA in New Zealand IS NOT A VOLCANO YET IT ERUPTED IN 1886 *SENDING A JET OF WATER MUD AND STONES 800 FEET INTO THE AIR AND CREATING A VAST CRATER*

THE GREAT REED
CUT OFF FROM THE SEA BY DRIFTING SAND, PROJECTS ROOTS AS FAR AS 30 FEET--*ALWAYS TOWARD THE NEAREST WATER*

WILLIAM WYKEHAM
(1324-1404)
THE ENGLISH CHANCELLOR INVITED 24 INDIGENTS *TO DINE WITH HIM EVERY DAY FOR 36 YEARS*

STALAGMITES
IN THE CAVE OF BOURNILLON, FRANCE, FORM WHAT APPEARS TO BE AN ENTIRE VILLAGE OF *NATIVE HUTS*

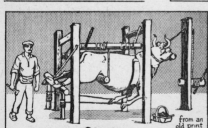

from an old print

COWS
ON MANY FARMS IN 19th-CENTURY FRANCE, TO MAKE IT EASIER FOR THEM TO WALK ON SOFT GROUND, WERE SHOD WITH HORSESHOES

THE *YOUNG* **LARVA** OF THE AFRICAN GRASSHOPPER PROTECTS ITSELF FROM PREDATORS BY LOOKING AMAZINGLY *LIKE AN ANT*

MISSISSIPPI BAY
IS LOCATED IN
JAPAN
THE BAY OF YEDO HAD
ITS NAME CHANGED
AFTER PERRY'S FLAGSHIP,
THE "MISSISSIPPI",
ANCHORED THERE ON
THE VOYAGE THAT
OPENED JAPAN TO
WESTERN SHIPPING

THE **WALKING FILE CABINET**
FRANCESCO PETRARCH (1304-1374)
THE CELEBRATED ITALIAN POET
THOUGHT OF IDEAS FOR HIS POEMS
WHILE WALKING AND JOTTED
THEM DOWN ON SLIPS OF PAPER
-- *WHICH HE ALWAYS
PINNED ON HIS ROBE*
HE NEVER RETURNED HOME UNTIL
HIS COAT WAS COVERED WITH NOTES

THE **GREAT CASTLE of HIROSAKI**
in Japan
HAS STOOD FOR MORE THAN 300 YEARS
- YET ITS FOUNDATION CONSISTS
ONLY OF A PILE OF LOOSE
STONES WITHOUT MORTAR

GUGLIELMO CACCIA
(1568-1625)
CELEBRATED ITALIAN PAINTER, WAS THE FATHER OF 5 DAUGHTERS WHO WERE TALENTED ARTISTS--BUT TO KEEP THEM FROM FOLLOWING THAT PROFESSION HE FOUNDED A CONVENT IN MONCALVA, ITALY, *IN WHICH ALL OF HIS DAUGHTERS BECAME NUNS*

THE CHURCH OF ST. MARTIN in Renaix, Belgium, *WAS CONVERTED INTO A GARAGE*

A LIVE CATFISH
WAS FOUND BY LUMBERMEN in Tuscarawas Park, in New Philadelphia, Ohio, IN A WATER-FILLED DEPRESSION IN A TREE *40 FEET ABOVE THE GROUND*— THE FISH WAS DROPPED INTO A LAKE AND SWAM AWAY

THE CASTLE OF CATAJO, Mezzavia, Italy, ONE OF ITALY'S MOST UNUSUAL STRUCTURES, WAS BUILT IN THE 16TH CENTURY FROM PLANS *BROUGHT BACK FROM CATHAY IN THE 13TH CENTURY BY MARCO POLO*

THE MALE OEKETICUS BAGWORM of So. America BUILDS A SILKEN COCOON WHICH SERVES FIRST AS A HATCHING PLACE FOR ITS BROOD *AND THEN AS A COFFIN FOR ITS MATE*

GIUSEPPE CADES (1750-1799)

WAS SO SKILLFUL A FORGER OF FAMOUS PAINTINGS THAT TO WIN A BET HE COPIED A PICTURE BY RAPHAEL AND SOLD IT FOR 500 GOLD SEQUINS TO C.A. CASANOVA, DIRECTOR OF THE DRESDEN CABINET --- *THE MOST CELEBRATED RAPHAELITE EXPERT OF HIS TIME-* CADES OFFERED TO REFUND THE MONEY BUT CASANOVA REFUSED TO ACKNOWLEDGE THAT HE HAD BEEN DECEIVED

THE HETERCYATHUS POLYP FOUND ON THE SHORE OF THE INDIAN OCEAN, SHARES AN ABANDONED SNAIL SHELL WITH THE ASPIDOSIPHON WORM--*THE POLYP GUARDING THE WORM AGAINST PREDATORS AND THE WORM PROVIDING TRANSPORTATION*

JEAN-GUERIN AFFRET

OF QUIBERON, FRANCE, SUMMONED TO THE PENSION OFFICE IN ETEL TO PROVE THAT HE WAS STILL ALIVE AND ENTITLED TO THE PENSION, *WALKED THE ENTIRE 25 MILES AT THE AGE OF 100*

AARON BURR WHO KILLED ALEXANDER HAMILTON IN A DUEL IN 1804, INTERCEDED TO PREVENT A DUEL BETWEEN HAMILTON AND JAMES MONROE IN 1797 —AN ACT THAT MAY HAVE SAVED HAMILTON'S LIFE

SANTA CLAUS THE CAVE OF DARGILAN, near Meyrueis, France, NATURAL STALAGMITE FORMATION

THE CORPSE THAT FOUND ITS WAY HOME
ANNE GOURLAY, A PASSENGER ON THE SCHOONER "CLAIRE CLARENDON" WHEN IT WAS WRECKED OFF THE ISLE OF WIGHT IN 1836, WAS DROWNED, BUT HER BODY WAS CARRIED 50 MILES BY THE TIDES —AND DEPOSITED ON THE BEACH IN FRONT OF HER FATHER'S COTTAGE

THE CATHEDRAL of BARCELONA
in Spain, WAS STARTED IN 1249 AND
NOT COMPLETED UNTIL 1913
664 YEARS LATER

TADEUSZ CZACKI
(1765-1813)
A POLISH PHILANTHROPIST
BECAUSE RUSSIANS HAD
FORBIDDEN ESTABLISHMENT
OF PUBLIC SCHOOLS IN HIS
COUNTRY, CREATED 126
SCHOOLS SECRETLY AT
HIS OWN EXPENSE
*--SPENDING THE EQUIVALENT
TODAY OF $10,000,000--*
BECAUSE WRITTEN RECORDS
WOULD HAVE BETRAYED HIM,
HE MADE ALL PAYROLL AND
MAINTENANCE PAYMENTS
BY MEMORY ALONE

THE
**AFRICAN
RAGWORT**
WITHSTANDS LONG
PERIODS OF DROUGHT
*BY HOARDING WATER
IN ITS LEAVES*

THE
**RIGHT
HAND**
OF EUGENE H. SLOANE, of Annapolis, Md.,
HAS VEINS WHICH DISTINCTLY
FORM THE INITIALS "MR"
SLOANE MARRIED A GIRL NAMED
MARGARET RILEY

THE
**WATER
SHREW**
SEEMS TO SHOW AFFECTION
FOR ITS OFFSPRING IN
CAREFULLY COACHING
THEM --BUT WHEN THEY
*ARE DISOBEDIENT
SHE DEVOURS THEM*

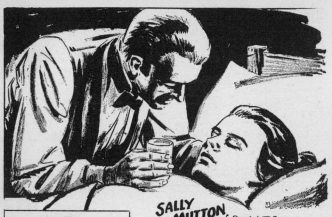

SALLY MUTTON of Bristol, R.I., WAS PRONOUNCED DEAD IN 1900, BUT HER HUSBAND REFUSED TO ACCEPT THE DOCTOR'S STATEMENT —AND HELD OFF THE UNDERTAKER WITH A SHOTGUN

HE POURED HOT MILK BETWEEN HIS WIFE'S LIPS —AND SHE REGAINED CONSCIOUSNESS AND SURVIVED HER HUSBAND BY 40 YEARS

HYPODERMA DIANA A European fly, HAS A FACE LIKE A MONKEY

THE **STARFISH FLOWER** (Stapelia gigantea) of South Africa LOOKS LIKE A STARFISH ENWRAPPED IN WEEDS

HOUSES on the island of Sumba, Indonesia, HAVE HOLLOW, POINTED ROOFS TO PROVIDE *LIVING QUARTERS FOR THE SPIRITS OF DEPARTED RELATIVES*

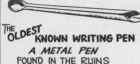

THE OLDEST KNOWN WRITING PEN

A METAL PEN FOUND IN THE RUINS OF POMPEII, ITALY, AND CONSISTING OF A ROLLED SHEET OF METAL AND A SPLIT NIB *WAS CONSTRUCTED 1,900 YEARS AGO*

HOW TO KEEP A CENSUS UP TO DATE

HOMES OCCUPIED BY MINANGKUBAU TRIBESMEN OF SUMATRA *ADD AN ADDITIONAL POINT TO THEIR ROOF EACH TIME A NEW BABY IS BORN*

THE MILLIPEDE of Southern Africa THE NAME OF WHICH SUGGESTS IT HAS 1,000 FEET *ACTUALLY HAS 320 FEET*

THE NEW WORLD WAS FOUNDED ON Christmas Eve!
THE SANTA MARIA, FLAGSHIP OF CHRISTOPHER COLUMBUS, WAS WRECKED OFF CAP-HAITIEN, HAITI, ON DECEMBER 24th, 1492, AND HIS MEN SET TO WORK IMMEDIATELY TO BUILD A FORT -- WHICH BECAME *THE FIRST PERMANENT SETTLEMENT IN AMERICA !*

NATIVES OF THE **JUNAG TRIBE** Orissa, India, BUILD COMFORTABLE HOMES, BUT THEY SLEEP OUTSIDE ON THE GROUND *AND THE HOUSES ARE OCCUPIED BY THEIR GOATS*

JOHN ERICSSON
(1803-1889)
The famed naval engineer
WAS OFFICIAL DRAFTSMAN OF THE SWEDISH CANAL COMPANY **AT THE AGE OF 12**
HE HEADED A LABOR FORCE OF 400 MEN IN THE CONSTRUCTION OF SWEDEN'S GÖTA CANAL WHEN HE WAS ONLY 14

HORSEBOATS —FLAT-BOTTOMED CRAFT 40 FEET LONG WERE USED FOR YEARS ON THE ALLAGASH RIVER IN MAINE—AND THE HORSES THAT PULLED THE BOATS UPRIVER ALWAYS *RODE BACK DOWNRIVER AS PASSENGERS*

THE **COLUMNS** WHICH LINE THE FRONT OF THE BROADWELL HOUSE, IN CINCINNATI, OHIO, EACH CONSIST OF THE *ENTIRE TRUNK OF A TREE*

A **KEY** USED IN OLDEN TIMES THAT *DOUBLED AS A PISTOL*

ARAB WOMEN MAY STOOP AT THEIR WORK *-BUT ARE FORBIDDEN TO KNEEL*

THE **PRESIDENT** OF ALGERIA USES THE NAME HOUARI BOUMEDIENNE *--BUT THIS IS AN ALIAS AND HE HAS NEVER REVEALED HIS REAL IDENTITY*

HOW A BEETLE MADE **5** CROSSINGS OF A ROUND TILE, EACH OF EQUAL LENGTH, AND ENDED UP EXACTLY AT ITS STARTING POINT

THE LIBRARY THAT STUBBORNNESS BUILT!

THE MILFORD LIBRARY IN Milford, Ohio, WAS CONSTRUCTED IN THE EARLY 19TH CENTURY BY JOHN KUGLER, THE CITY'S WEALTHIEST RESIDENT, FROM STONES HE HAD COLLECTED TO BUILD A PRIVATE BRIDGE ACROSS THE MIAMI RIVER--*BECAUSE HE REFUSED TO PAY A TOLL ON THE CITY'S SPAN*

THE COMMUNITY ACCEPTED THE LIBRARY IN LIEU OF TOLLS

A **PICTORIAL ALPHABET** WAS CREATED FOR THE MICMAC INDIANS OF THE GULF OF ST. LAWRENCE BY CHRISTIAN KAUDER, AN AUSTRIAN MISSIONARY, *TO PROVIDE THEM WITH A BIBLE*

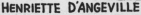

HENRIETTE D'ANGEVILLE

AFTER CLIMBING MONT BLANC, EUROPE'S HIGHEST MOUNTAIN, MADE CERTAIN THAT SHE WOULD ESTABLISH A NEW RECORD AT THE 15,771-FOOT-HIGH PEAK BY *CLIMBING ONTO THE SHOULDERS OF HER GUIDES* (Sept. 4, 1838)

HOLY MEN of the Jaina Sect of India NEVER WEAR SHOES, EAT NOTHING BETWEEN SUNSET AND SUNRISE, AND CAN SHAPE THEIR HAIR AND BEARDS ONLY BY PLUCKING THE HAIR OUT BY THE ROOTS—

THEY NEVER LIGHT A FIRE LEST IT HARM INSECTS, AND BANDAGE THEIR MOUTHS TO PREVENT THEM FROM *INHALING -AND HARMING- GERMS AND FLIES*

THE MURDER INN of Berlin, Germany, WAS GIVEN THAT NAME AS A WHIM BY ITS FOUNDER -YET IN LESS THAN A YEAR *THE OWNER AND HIS ENTIRE FAMILY WERE MURDERED* (1837)

LUCAS **C**ORNELISZ (1495-1552) CELEBRATED DUTCH PAINTER WAS KNOWN AS "THE COOK" BECAUSE WHEN BUSINESS WAS SLOW IN ART, *HE WORKED AS A CHEF*

THE **STREETS** on the island of Sein, France, WERE CONSTRUCTED JUST WIDE ENOUGH TO ENABLE ITS INHABITANTS TO ROLL *BARRELS OF FISH THROUGH THEM*

THE **GREAT TEMPLE GATE** of Shravanbelgola, India, WAS CARVED FROM A *SINGLE BLOCK OF GRANITE*

NICCOLO CACCIATORE
⟨ 1780-1841 ⟩
WAS PROFESSOR OF GREEK AT THE UNIVERSITY OF GIRGENTI, SICILY, *AT THE AGE OF 16*

CHANGE THIS TRIANGLE TO A SQUARE COVERING EXACTLY HALF THE TRIANGLE'S AREA, BY MEANS OF A SINGLE, STRAIGHT CUT. Solution: FOLD TRIANGLE AS INDICATED IN 1 AND 2. FOLD IT AGAIN FROM RIGHT TO LEFT, CREATING SHAPE 3. WITH A SINGLE, STRAIGHT CUT OF THE SHEARS, SLICE AWAY "A" AND OPEN THE FOLDED PAPER

THE **EAGLE RAY** of the Mediterranean, WHICH HAS A HIGHLY POISONOUS STING IN ITS TAIL, *LOOKS REMARKABLY LIKE A SOARING EAGLE*

VALTETSI a village in Greece **IS ABANDONED FOR 6 MONTHS EACH YEAR**

ITS 180 FAMILIES LEAVE IN APRIL TO FIND NEW GRAZING GROUNDS FOR THEIR SHEEP AND DO NOT RETURN UNTIL OCTOBER

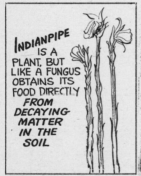

INDIANPIPE IS A PLANT, BUT LIKE A FUNGUS OBTAINS ITS FOOD DIRECTLY *FROM DECAYING MATTER IN THE SOIL*

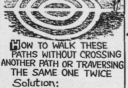

HOW TO WALK THESE PATHS WITHOUT CROSSING ANOTHER PATH OR TRAVERSING THE SAME ONE TWICE

Solution:

CAMILLE DUJOUR (1812-1872) of Besançon, France, WHOSE LAST NAME IN FRENCH MEANS "OF THE DAY" NAMED HIS **4** CHILDREN

MATIN, FOR "MORNING"
MIDI, FOR "NOON"
SOIR, FOR "EVENING"
NUIT, FOR "NIGHT"

FENCE POSTS IN THE SKY

THE JACKSON-HARMSWORTH POLAR EXPEDITION FOR A PERIOD OF 15 MINUTES OVER FRANZ JOSEF LAND IN THE ARCTIC, SAW THE SKY HEMMED IN BY WHAT APPEARED TO BE *THOUSANDS OF INTERLACED POSTS*

ELISABETH KULMANN

(1808-1825) of St. Petersburg, Russia, BEFORE HER DEATH AT THE AGE OF 17 *HAD MASTERED 17 LANGUAGES --AND WROTE DISTINGUISHED POETRY IN 7 LANGUAGES*

ARTEMAS HOWE
WHO DIED A VICTIM OF HEART DISEASE IN 1840
HIS HEART IS NO LONGER THE SEAT OF TROUBLES, TORTURING PAIN
IT CEASED TO FLUTTER AND BEAT AND NEVER WILL FLUTTER AGAIN

Epitaph IN NORTH CEMETERY PRINCETON, MASS.

ZSCHOKKE ROCK

A BOULDER NEAR CASTLE ZWERNITZ, GERMANY, BEARS A REMARKABLE RESEMBLANCE TO *HEINRICH ZSCHOKKE, THE CELEBRATED SWISS NOVELIST*

A **Turkey** DOMINATES THE STRICKLAND CREST BECAUSE AN ANCESTOR BROUGHT HOME FROM SEBASTIAN CABOT'S EXPEDITION TO THE NEW WORLD IN 1524 *THE FIRST TURKEY EVER SEEN IN ENGLAND*

A **COW** FITTED BY DR. BYRON BERNARD, A VETERINARIAN OF PARK HILLS, KY., *WITH A STEEL PEG LEG*

THE **TREE DUCKS** of Panama PERCH AND NEST *IN TREES*

A **3-FOOT-GAUGE RAILROAD** OPERATED BY A LUMBER COMPANY IN TUOLUMNE COUNTY, CALIF., FOR YEARS USED AS ITS ROLLING STOCK ANCIENT *MOTOR CARS ADAPTED TO RUN ON THE RAILS*

THE JOB THAT HAD NO FUTURE

KYCHAN (1786-1852) WAS FIRED AS VICEROY OF HONAN, CHINA, BECAUSE HE FAILED TO PREDICT A FLOOD BY THE YELLOW RIVER, AND WAS EXECUTED SOME YEARS LATER BECAUSE AS VICEROY OF SZECHUAN IT WAS FELT THAT HE SHOULD HAVE FORESEEN *AN EARTHQUAKE THAT DEVASTATED THE PROVINCE*

179

A **HUNTING KNIFE**
OF 16th-CENTURY GERMANY
WHICH DOUBLED
AS A PISTOL

ROSSINI
(1792-1868)
THE ITALIAN COMPOSER BECAME SO STOUT IN HIS LATER YEARS THAT TO ACCOMMODATE HIS BULGING STOMACH *A HUGE PORTION HAD TO BE CUT OUT OF HIS DINING ROOM TABLE*

THE CASTLE OF GUÉRONNIÈRE
A MAGNIFICENT STRUCTURE IN LISSON, FRANCE, WAS SOLD BY THE GOVERNMENT DURING THE FRENCH REVOLUTION FOR ~~$15~~ —
THE HIGH BIDDER WAS A SERVANT OF THE ORIGINAL OWNER -- WHO GAVE IT BACK TO HIM AFTER THE REVOLUTION

MONTEMALE CASTLE
LOCATED ON A HILL NEAR CUNEO, ON THE ITALIAN-FRENCH FRONTIER, COULD NOT BE SOLD BY ITS OWNERS IN 1933 *ALTHOUGH ITS PRICE WAS REDUCED TO 7 LIRE--* (35 CENTS)

THE CONDEMNED MAN WHO LIVED TO GET THE LAST LAUGH

BARON IMHOFF (1705-1751) WAS ARRESTED BY THE GOVERNOR GENERAL OF THE DUTCH EAST INDIES IN 1740 AND DEPORTED TO AMSTERDAM TO BE EXECUTED FOR TREASON --BUT INSTEAD IMHOFF WAS SENT BACK TO BATAVIA, IN THE DUTCH EAST INDIES, *TO REPLACE HIS ACCUSER AS GOVERNOR GENERAL*

THE FIRST "AUTOMOBILE"

A MECHANICAL CARRIAGE, THE PROPULSION POWER FOR WHICH WAS NEVER REVEALED, WAS DRIVEN THROUGH THE CITY GATE OF MEMMINGEN, GERMANY, *IN 1447*

JULIETTE DROUET
(1806-1882)
A FAMOUS FRENCH ACTRESS AT THE TIME SHE MET NOVELIST VICTOR HUGO --*WROTE HIM 20,000 LOVE LETTERS*

AN **ANCIENT STONE MEMORIAL** TO A PAGAN GOD STANDS IN THE CATHEDRAL OF LE MANS, FRANCE, *A SYMBOL OF CHRISTIANITY'S TRIUMPH OVER PAGANISM*

A PIECE OF FERRARA MARBLE

NOW IN THE MUSEUM OF NATURAL HISTORY IN LONDON, ENGLAND, IS SHAPED BY NATURE TO RESEMBLE A CITY SKYLINE *COMPLETE WITH SCORES OF SKYSCRAPERS AND 2 RIVERS*

FIELD MARSHAL LOUIS ANTOINE de BIRON
(1700-1788) of France
IN THE BATTLE OF FONTENOY, BELGIUM,
*HAD 5 HORSES SHOT DEAD BENEATH HIM
--YET HE ESCAPED WITHOUT A SCRATCH*

HOW TO CHANGE THE LETTER "S" INTO A SOLID CARTWHEEL BY A SINGLE CUT

Solution:

CUT THROUGH THE "S" AS INDICATED AND FILL IN THE HOLE IN THE CENTER OF THE CARTWHEEL WITH THE SHADED PORTIONS OF THE ORIGINAL SHAPE

ROAST CHICKENS
FOR THE TABLE OF KING LOUIS XIV OF FRANCE, WERE CARRIED THROUGH THE STREETS IN BASKETS EACH DAY
--AND EVERY PASSERBY WAS REQUIRED TO TIP HIS HAT AND BOW DEEPLY

HOW TO CARVE THIS BLOCK OF STONE TO FORM A SQUARE

Solution:

THE MEMORIAL TO A CAT

THE PET CAT OF PETRARCH, THE ITALIAN POET, WAS BURIED IN THE HOUSE OF ITS MASTER AT ARQUA, ITALY, BENEATH A GRAVESTONE ESPECIALLY CREATED BY *ONE OF ITALY'S MOST CELEBRATED ARTISTS, GIOTTO*

EDEN PARK DRIVE BRIDGE
in Cincinnati, Ohio,
BUILT BY AN AUSTRIAN ENGINEER IN 1894
WAS THE WORLD'S FIRST CONCRETE BRIDGE

BURL T. WOOD
MAKES HIS LIVING CARVING *WOOD BURLS*
Lindsay, Calif.

THE **PATROL** THAT WAS SAVED BY A WAD OF CHEWING TOBACCO

2 U.S. SCOUTS WRIGGLING THROUGH 1,000 HOSTILE INDIANS TO GET HELP FOR A FORCE OF CAVALRYMEN ON THE ARIKAREE FORK OF THE REPUBLICAN RIVER IN COLO., SUDDENLY FOUND THEIR PATH BLOCKED BY A RATTLESNAKE *COILED AND READY TO STRIKE!* UNABLE TO SHOOT THE RATTLER BECAUSE THE SOUND WOULD HAVE BROUGHT THE NEARBY CHEYENNE WARRIORS, SCOUT TRUDEAU DROVE OFF THE SNAKE *BY SQUIRTING IT WITH TOBACCO JUICE* (Sept. 17, 1868)

MARIE-MARGUERITE THEAULON
(1787- 1841) THE FRENCH DRAMATIST WROTE 50 THREE-ACT PLAYS EACH YEAR FOR 5 SUCCESSIVE YEARS-- *--YET DIED PENNILESS*

THE **INDIAN RED-WATTLED LAPWING** WHEN ALARMED ISSUES A CRY THAT SOUNDS LIKE *"DID HE DO IT?"*

THE CASTLE of **PONT-de-MARS**, FRANCE, WAS CONSTRUCTED IN 1928 ENTIRELY FROM *THE DEBRIS OF AN ANCIENT CASTLE THAT HAD COMPLETELY DISINTEGRATED*

DON CIMINO of Chicago, Ill., FROM A PLATE OF STEAMING ALPHABET SOUP SCOOPED UP A SPOONFUL THAT INCLUDED JUST 3 LETTERS--**HOT**

MOUNTAIN ROADS ON THE ISLAND OF MADEIRA ARE GOUGED FROM PRECIPICES *BY WORKMEN DANGLING ON ROPES 5,000 FEET ABOVE THE VALLEY FLOOR*

THE **MARQUIS LUIGI TORRIGIANI** OF FLORENCE, ITALY, BET HE COULD SHOOT 1,000 PIGEONS IN 12 HOURS AND ACTUALLY SHOT 850 -- *BUT LOST HIS BET BECAUSE HIS GUN BECAME SO HOT HE HAD TO COOL THE BARREL IN COLD WATER FOR PERIODS TOTALING 1½ HOURS*

LUIGI LABLACHE (1794-1858) A PROFESSIONAL CONTRALTO SANG SO LOUDLY AT THE AGE OF 17 THAT HIS VOCAL CORDS REMAINED PARALYZED FOR 2 MONTHS -- UNTIL A FIT OF COUGHING RESTORED HIS VOICE AND *HE BECAME A HIGHLY ACCLAIMED BASSO*

16	12		5		2	18
13	1			6		
			8			10
14	15		9			4
17	7		3	19		11

ARRANGE THESE NUMBERS SO THAT THE ROWS AND COLUMNS TOTAL **33**, SEVEN WAYS

Solution:

17	7	8 9	10	4	14	15
		3	19	11		
5	16	12		2	18	13
		1		6		

186

THE ENGADINE RAILROAD STATION In Michigan
WAS BUILT BY THE TOWNSPEOPLE IN 1888 WITHOUT PERMISSION FROM THE
RAILWAY *ON A SINGLE SUNDAY, BETWEEN DAWN AND DUSK*

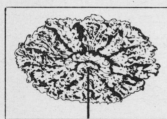

The **FLORAL
CEILING DECORATION**
IN THE PLANTATION HOUSE IN
BELLEVUE, MISSISSIPPI, IS STILL
PERFECTLY PRESERVED ALTHOUGH
*IT WAS MADE OF FINE PLASTER,
MARBLE DUST, COTTON, CHOPPED
STRAW, HONEY AND THE SAP
OF FIG TREES*

WOMEN OF THE BUSHMAN TRIBE CAN DRAW UP WATER THROUGH
HOLLOW REEDS **FROM BENEATH THE ARID SANDS OF AFRICA'S KALAHARI
DESERT** *--THEY SUCK UP THE WATER FROM BENEATH A SHRUB AND
SQUIRT IT THROUGH A 2nd REED INTO AN EMPTY OSTRICH EGG FOR STORAGE*

187

PAUL de KOCK (1793-1871)
THE CELEBRATED FRENCH NOVELIST,
SAVED HIS MOTHER'S LIFE
5 MONTHS BEFORE HE WAS BORN —
BOTH HIS PARENTS WERE SENTENCED
TO DEATH IN THE FRENCH
REVOLUTION, BUT THE MOTHER'S
EXECUTION WAS POSTPONED BECAUSE
SHE WAS CARRYING PAUL -- *AND
THE SENTENCE WAS LATER COMMUTED*

THE **BISHOP LIGHTHOUSE**
in the Scilly Isles
167 FEET HIGH AND
IN AN EXPOSED SPOT
*SWAYS LIKE A TREE
DURING STORMS*

THE **GRAVESTONES** of ESA TRIBESMEN,
in Somaliland,
COMPRISE A LINE OF ROCKS IN THE
SHAPE OF A HORSESHOE -- INSIDE OF
WHICH ARE 3 MINIATURE STONE HUTS
COMMEMORATING THE DECEASED'S 3
WIVES, AND OUTSIDE OF WHICH IS
*ONE STONE FOR EACH ENEMY HE
KILLED DURING HIS LIFETIME*

THE **OFFICIAL SEAL**
of the Rational College
of Milan, Italy,
FEATURED **3**
MATHEMATICAL FORMULAS
*CONSIDERED MAGICAL AIDS
TO SUCCESS--THE DOUBLING,
TRIPLING AND SEXTUPLING
OF THE FIGURE ONE*

THE CITY EMBLEM
of Aussig, Czechoslovakia,
DEPICTS A MAN RAISING A
CLUB AND CARRIES THE WORDS:
"He who gives his children bread
And suffers want in old age
I kill him with my cudgel"

JEAN OTTER (1707-1748)
A NATIVE OF SWEDEN WHO SETTLED
IN PARIS, FRANCE, IN 1733,
IN A SINGLE YEAR AND WITH-
OUT A TEACHER MASTERED
FRENCH, ENGLISH, SPANISH,
ITALIAN, DANISH AND GERMAN
*SENT TO THE FAR EAST BY
THE FRENCH GOVERNMENT HE
LEARNED 10 ORIENTAL LANGUAGES
--AND UPON HIS RETURN
BECAME PROFESSOR OF ARABIC
AT THE UNIVERSITY OF PARIS*

**DYAK
WOMEN**
of
Borneo
WEAR
EARRINGS
THAT
WEIGH
**5
POUNDS**

AUGUSTE JEGUREL
A SOLDIER FROM QUIBERON, FRANCE, LOST BOTH LEGS IN THE FRANCO-PRUSSIAN WAR OF 1870 AND WAS OFFICIALLY DECLARED DEAD --*BUT 44 YEARS LATER THE GOVERNMENT LEARNED HE WAS ALIVE AND AWARDED HIM THE MEDAILLE MILITAIRE*

THE **HUTS** OF NATIVES IN THE ARUWIMI SECTION OF THE CONGO HAVE GIGANTIC STEEPLES MADE OF BRUSH AND LEAVES -*WHICH MAKE THEM LOOK LIKE A FOREST OF MAJESTIC CYPRESS TREES*

A
WEAPON
USED IN INDIA
IN THE 19th CENTURY
-*COMBINING A
DAGGER AND 2 PISTOLS*

LAKE PROVIDENCE
IN EAST CARROLL PARISH, LA., *IS SHAPED LIKE A HORSESHOE*

LAUGHING DEATH

IS A DISEASE THAT
OCCURS IN THE FORE
VALLEY OF NEW GUINEA
--AND *NOWHERE ELSE
IN THE WORLD*

THE PROPHETIC TOWER

THE **TOWER** of the
CHURCH of St. KATHARINE, in Hamburg,
Germany, WAS DEDICATED UPON ITS
COMPLETION BY KING CHRISTIAN IV OF
DENMARK, TO WHOM THE GRATEFUL
BUILDER WISHED A LIFE *"THAT SHALL
ENDURE AS LONG AS THIS TOWER"*-
THE TOWER WAS DEMOLISHED BY A
STORM ON FEB. 28, 1648 --*AND KING
CHRISTIAN DIED THAT SAME NIGHT*

HOW TO
DIVIDE
THIS SAUSAGE
INTO **10** PARTS
WITH **3** CUTS

Solution: CUT IT IN HALF, LENGTHWISE,
BY A SINGLE STROKE, THEN WITH
ONE HALF RESTING ON THE OTHER
CUT TWICE THROUGH BOTH
PIECES AS INDICATED

MEXICAN
OROPENDOLAS

AS A PROTECTION
AGAINST PREDATORS
ALWAYS BUILD
THEIR 6-FOOT-
LONG NESTS
*ALONGSIDE THE
NESTS OF WASPS*

POINTED HUTS

CONSTRUCTED BY THE ANCIENT CELTS NEAR FORCALQUIER, FRANCE, WERE BUILT OF STONE WITHOUT THE USE OF MORTAR--YET THEY STILL STAND AFTER *20* CENTURIES

JOHN DAVID ZERKO

of Orange, Texas, AS A STUDENT IN ELEMENTARY SCHOOL, JUNIOR HIGH, HIGH SCHOOL AND JUNIOR COLLEGE *HAD A PERFECT ATTENDANCE RECORD FOR 14 YEARS*

Wedding Invitations IN FINKENWERDER, GERMANY, FOR CENTURIES WERE DELIVERED ORALLY BY MESSENGERS WHO, TO MOVE MORE SWIFTLY, *ALWAYS TRAVELED ON STILTS*

SINGLE GIRLS

IN HARRAR, ETHIOPIA, ADVERTISE THEIR ELIGIBILITY BY WEARING *RED SKIRTS WITH BLUE DOTS* --WHILE MARRIED WOMEN WEAR *BLUE SKIRTS WITH RED DOTS*